英文E-mail
写作100主题

100 Topics
for E-mail
Writing

[加] Matthew Trueman 著

葛欣 王欢 译

外文出版社
FOREIGN LANGUAGES PRESS

前言

　　快速,是 E-mail 沟通的最大特点。一些要紧的事情往往需要你在几分钟之内回应对方。如果这时你的英文跟不上,是不是很抓狂?

　　如果你因此下定决心提高英文写作能力,买回一本书从头学起,很快你就会更抓狂:"我不要学那么多,我只是需要临时应对的几句话!"

　　你眼前的这本书,《英文 E-mail 写作 100 主题》将以简单、快捷的方式帮助你解决语言难题。这里不仅有"临时应对的那几句",还有更多更好的选择——

　　每个话题下面有两篇信例。话题 1-76 的信例分为"生活类"和"商务类",话题 77 之后全部是商务、申请类信例。

　　每个话题下面有丰富的例句。如果信例不能确切表达你的意思,你可以从例句中寻找更贴切的语句。

　　此外,本书的英文新鲜、地道、生动,能解除你"中式英语"和"古旧英语"的隐忧。

祝你好运!

作　者

Contents
目　录

第一部分　友好往来

1. 邮件常用语（告知，附件，回复，问询）…………………… 1
2. 问候 ……………………………… 4
3. 表示感谢 ………………………… 6
4. 祝愿和祝贺 ……………………… 8
5. 道歉 ……………………………… 12
6. 表示慰问 ………………………… 14
7. 约定时间/计划 …………………… 16
8. 询问联系方式 …………………… 19
9. 告知消息 ………………………… 21

第二部分　提出想法

10. 邀请 ……………………………… 23
11. 提醒 ……………………………… 26
12. 请求帮助 ………………………… 27
13. 提供帮助 ………………………… 29
14. 建议 ……………………………… 30
15. 警告 ……………………………… 32
16. 劝说 ……………………………… 34

第三部分　表明态度

17. 表达愿望 ………………………… 36
18. 说明意向 ………………………… 37
19. 表达重要性 ……………………… 38
20. 表示有能力 ……………………… 40
21. 请求许可 ………………………… 41
22. 应该不应该 ……………………… 44
23. 赞同和不赞同 …………………… 45
24. 喜欢和不喜欢 …………………… 47
25. 表示偏爱 ………………………… 49
26. 表示兴趣 ………………………… 50
27. 表示不确定 ……………………… 52

28. 责怪和抱怨 ……………………… 54

第四部分　可能程度

29. 肯定和不肯定 …………………… 56
30. 可能和不可能 …………………… 57
31. 猜测 ……………………………… 59

第五部分　表达情感

32. 惊讶 ……………………………… 61
33. 好奇 ……………………………… 62
34. 高兴 ……………………………… 64
35. 赞赏 ……………………………… 65
36. 自信 ……………………………… 66
37. 鼓励 ……………………………… 67
38. 关心 ……………………………… 69
39. 后悔 ……………………………… 71
40. 生气 ……………………………… 72
41. 担心 ……………………………… 74
42. 害怕 ……………………………… 75

第六部分　论证观点

43. 例证 ……………………………… 77
44. 分类 ……………………………… 78
45. 比较和对比 ……………………… 79
46. 概括 ……………………………… 81
47. 推断 ……………………………… 83
48. 阐明 ……………………………… 84
49. 结论 ……………………………… 85

第七部分　说明时间

50. 时刻 ……………………………… 87
51. 频度 ……………………………… 88
52. 时序和顺序 ……………………… 89
53. 速度 ……………………………… 91

54. 同时 …………………… 92
55. 持续 …………………… 94

第八部分　描述空间

56. 位置 …………………… 95
57. 方向 …………………… 96
58. 距离 …………………… 97
59. 面积和体积 …………… 98

第九部分　说明数量

60. 数 ……………………… 100
61. 量 ……………………… 101
62. 足量和不足量 ………… 102
63. 过量 …………………… 104

第十部分　说明性质

64. 形状 …………………… 106
65. 颜色 …………………… 107
66. 材料 …………………… 108
67. 感觉 …………………… 109
68. 质地 …………………… 111
69. 价值 …………………… 112

第十一部分　说明数值

70. 基础运算 ……………… 114
71. 倍数和百分比 ………… 115
72. 增加和减少 …………… 116
73. 基础测量（长、宽等）… 118
74. 近似值和平均值 ……… 119
75. 比率和比例 …………… 121
76. 最大值和最小值 ……… 122

第十二部分　通知

77. 通知开会 ……………… 124
78. 更改开会时间 ………… 125
79. 通知做预算 …………… 126
80. 申请购买办公用品 …… 127
81. 通知放假 ……………… 129
82. 晚会通知 ……………… 130

83. 通知人事更换 ………… 131

第十三部分　访问事宜

84. 约定来访时间 ………… 133
85. 欢迎来访 ……………… 134
86. 更改来访时间 ………… 135
87. 预订房间 ……………… 136
88. 感谢热情接待 ………… 138

第十四部分　组织会议

89. 邀请 …………………… 140
90. 回复邀请 ……………… 141
91. 会后交流 ……………… 143

第十五部分　贸易往来

92. 咨询公司信息 ………… 144
93. 介绍公司 ……………… 145
94. 询问产品信息 ………… 146
95. 介绍产品及报价 ……… 148
96. 讨价还价 ……………… 150
97. 下订单 ………………… 151
98. 确认订单 ……………… 153
99. 催货 …………………… 154
100. 为交货延迟而道歉 …… 156
101. 催货款 ………………… 157
102. 请求延期付款 ………… 158

第十六部分　申请信函

103. 申请职位/求职 ……… 160
104. 推荐信 ………………… 162
105. 申请留学 ……………… 164

附　录

常用连接词
商务书信常用表达法
公司职位名称
公司部门名称
常用信尾结束语
常用 E-mail 表情符号

第一部分　友好往来
Personal Correspondence

1　邮件常用语 Common e-mail language

告知　*Providing information*

❶ My new e-mail address is.... 　　　我的新邮箱地址是……

❷ I've forwarded your e-mail to.... 　　　我已经把你的邮件转发给……

❸ Please e-mail or call to confirm. 　　　请邮件或电话确认。

❹ Please visit us on the web at http://www.... 　　　请登陆我们的网站，地址是……

❺ Please visit our new website at http://www.... 　　　请登陆我们的新网站……

❻ This is just a test message to see whether you can receive my e-mails. 　　　这条信息只是想试一下您是否能收到我的邮件。

❼ I sent you the magazine that you wanted to borrow. 　　　我给你寄去了你想借的杂志。

❽ You should receive it by Friday at the latest. 　　　您最迟在周五收到。

❾ Please return it to me when you're done with it. 　　　请您用完后还给我。

❿ I tried calling you at that number, but the line was busy. 　　　我给你打这个号码，但是占线。

⓫ I'll be away from the office tomorrow. 　　　我明天不在办公室。

附件　*Attachments*

❶ Please find attached a copy of the file you requested. 　　　请在附件中查收您要的那份文件。

❷ Please let me know whether you're able to open the attachment. 　　　请告知您是否能够打开附件。

❸ Please let me know if you've received the attachment. 　　　请告知您是否收到附件。

❹ I was unable to open the attached file. 　　　我不能打开附件。

❺ I think you might have sent the wrong attachment. 　　　我想您的附件可能发错了。

⑥ I was able to open the attached document, but there was a problem with the format. 　我能打开附件，但格式有问题。

⑦ Please resend the file in plain text format. 　请以纯文本格式再发送一遍文件。

⑧ Please try sending the attachment again. 　请再发送一遍附件。

⑨ I'm attaching the report in two different file formats. 　在附件中，我用两种不同的文件格式给您发了报告。

⑩ For some reason, I didn't receive the file attachment. 　由于某种原因我没能收到附件。

回复 Replying

❶ Thank you for your e-mail/message. 　谢谢您的来信。

❷ Thank you for your inquiry. 　感谢您的咨询。

❸ Thank you for your reply. 　谢谢您的回信。

❹ I'm glad to hear that you're doing well. 　知道你一切都好，我很高兴。

❺ It's good to know that everything is going well at your end. 　得知你一切顺利，我很高兴。

❻ I'll try to answer each of your questions one by one. 　我会按顺序回答您的每个问题。

❼ Please let me know if you have any further questions. 　请告知您是否还有其他问题。

❽ Please visit the websites below for additional information on this topic. 　请登陆下面的网站查询有关这个话题的更多信息。

❾ I have directed your inquiry to our technical staff. 　我已经把你的问题转给我们的技术人员。

❿ I forwarded your e-mail to my business partner. 　我已经把你的邮件转发给我的商业伙伴了。

⓫ I'll contact you as soon as I receive his reply. 　我一收到他的回信就跟你联系。

⓬ Write back when you get a chance and let me know what's new. 　有空给我写信，告诉我你的近况如何。

⓭ Keep/stay in touch! 　保持联系！

问询 Making inquiries

❶ Did you receive the e-mail that I sent a few days ago? 　我几天前发给你的邮件你收到了吗？

❷ I wasn't sure whether you got it, so I just wanted to check.

我不知道你收没收到，所以我只是想确认一下。

❸ Have you received my postcard yet?

你收到我的明信片了吗？

❹ Is it possible to reset my password to log into your website?

我能重新设置密码登陆你们的网站吗？

❺ Please confirm whether you have received the itinerary for Friday's meeting.

请确认你是否已经收到周五会议的日程安排。

❻ Please let me know as soon as possible.

请尽快告知。

❼ Did you finish writing the report yet?

你写完报告了吗？

❽ What are your plans for this weekend?

这周末你有什么计划呢？

❾ I would like to hear any suggestions you might have.

我想听听你的建议。

信例1（生活类）

Hey Mike,

How have you been lately? I just wanted to let you know that I switched to a new e-mail account. Look under "Sender" and you should be able to see my new e-mail address. I'll keep checking my old inbox, but you can e-mail me at the new address from now on.

Keep in touch,

Timothy

最近怎么样？我就是想告诉你我换新邮箱了。在寄件人下面你能看到我的新邮箱地址。我还会继续查看我以前的收件箱，不过以后你就往我的新邮箱发邮件吧。

信例2（商务类）

Dear Joe,

Thank you for your reply. I really appreciate you working late yesterday to finish the proposal. Unfortunately, I wasn't able to open the file attachment for some reason. Could you try saving it in plain text format and resending it? Looking forward to seeing you at next week's meeting.

Best regards,

Margaret

非常感谢你的回信，你为了完成提案昨天工作到那么晚我不甚感激，可惜的是不知道什么原因我无法打开附件。你能以纯文本形式保存这份文件，再给我发一次吗？期盼着在下周的会议上能与你见面。

② 问候 Greetings

询问近况 *Asking the other's situation*

❶ How are you? 你(您)好吗?

❷ How are things going? 最近怎么样?

❸ How is everything? 最近好吗?

❹ How's everything at your end? 你那边怎么样?

❺ What's new? 你怎么样?/你可好?

❻ What's up? 出什么事了?/怎么啦?

❼ What are you up to? 你最近忙什么呢?

❽ What have you been up to recently? 你最近忙什么呢?

❾ What's going on? 出什么事了?

❿ How's your school/university life going? 学校/大学生活怎么样?

⓫ How did your exam(s) go? 你考试考得怎么样?

⓬ I'm sure you did an excellent job. 我相信你做得很出色。

⓭ I hope you had a pleasant/relaxing holiday. 希望你度过了一个愉快/轻松的假期。

⓮ I hope all is well with you and your family. 希望你们全家平安。

说明近况 *Describing one's situation*

❶ I'm doing alright/fine/okay. 我还行。/我还好。

❷ I'm doing very well. 我挺好的。

❸ I'm keeping very busy. 我一直很忙。

❹ I'm keeping myself busy with my studies. 我学习很忙。/我一直忙于学习。

❺ I'm keeping myself busy as usual. 我还像往常那么忙。

❻ Everything is fine/okay. 一切都好。

❼ Everything is going very well. 一切都很好。

❽ Everything is pretty much the same as usual. 一切基本上和往常一样。

❾ Not much is new here. 这边没有什么新鲜事。

说明身体状况 *Describing one's health*

❶ I'm not feeling very well. 我身体不是很好。

❷ I think I need a few days off. 我觉得我得请几天假。

❸ I really need some R&R (rest and relaxation). 　　我真的需要休息，好好放松一下。

❹ I've caught a cold. 　　我感冒了。

❺ I have a sore throat. 　　我嗓子疼。

❻ I'm feeling nauseous today. 　　我今天有点儿恶心。

❼ I think I have a slight fever. 　　我觉得我有点儿发烧。

❽ I've been feeling under the weather all day. 　　我一整天都感觉不舒服。

❾ I've been feeling lethargic lately. 　　我最近总昏昏沉沉的。

❿ I've been sick for over a week now. 　　我生病一周多了。

⓫ I can barely get out of bed. 　　我差一点儿起不来床。

⓬ I have a pain in my chest/stomach/back/head/neck/throat. 　　我胸口疼/胃疼/背疼/头疼/脖子疼/嗓子疼。

⓭ My chest/stomach/back/head/neck/throat hurts. 　　我胸口疼/胃疼/背疼/头疼/脖子疼/嗓子疼。

⓮ I have a bit of a (an) headache/stomachache/earache/toothache. 　　我有点儿头痛/胃痛/耳朵痛/牙痛。

⓯ I'm finally starting to get better. 　　我终于开始好转了。

⓰ I've regained my strength/energy. 　　我恢复了体力/精力。

⓱ I've gained/lost some weight. 　　我体重增加了/我体重减轻了。

⓲ I've lost over 5 pounds since getting sick. 　　自从生病，我瘦了5磅多。

⓳ I feel a whole lot better today. 　　我今天觉得好多了。

⓴ I've never felt better. 　　我一直都没好转。

信例1（生活类）

Hi Tony,

How's your vacation going? You must be having an awesome time in Europe! Which countries have you visited so far? I got a part-time job as a waitress and I'm enjoying it so far. Anyway, we all miss you and can't wait to see you when you get back. Be sure to write soon.

Best wishes,

Gabriela

假期过得怎么样？你在欧洲一定是过得惊心动魄吧。到现在为止你都去过哪些国家了？我找了份兼职做服务员，过得很开心。不管怎么说我们很想你，已经等不及你回来看你了。一定要给我们写信！

Dear Jake,

I was so glad to receive your letter. It's been about two weeks since I was transferred to our southwestern branch. The office is a bit smaller and I'm still getting used to the new environment, but my new colleagues are all very friendly. How's everything going at your end?

Warm regards,

Grace

很高兴收到你的来信。我调到西南分公司已经有两周了。虽然办公室有点儿小，而且我还在适应新环境，但我的新同事都非常友好。你那边怎么样，一切顺利吗？

3 表示感谢 Expressing thanks

❶	Thanks so much.	多谢。
❷	Thank you very much.	非常感谢。
❸	Thank you for the beautiful gift/present/ card/flowers.	感谢你的礼物/贺卡/花。
❹	Thank you for the blue sweater you sent me for my birthday.	感谢你送给我的生日礼物蓝色毛衣。
❺	Thank you for the information on your products.	感谢你的产品信息。
❻	Thank you for being so considerate.	感谢你这样体贴。
❼	Thank you for the invitation.	谢谢你的邀请。
❽	Thank you for all your help.	谢谢你的帮助。
❾	Thank you again for your kindness and caring.	再次感谢你的好意和关心。
❿	Thank you for everything.	谢谢你为我做的这一切。
⓫	Thank you so much for everything.	非常感谢你为我做的这一切。
⓬	Thanks again for everything!	再次感谢你做的这一切。
⓭	Thanks for helping me move yesterday!	谢谢你昨天帮我搬家。
⓮	Thanks for all your efforts.	谢谢你所做出的努力。
⓯	It was so thoughtful of you.	你真体贴人。
⓰	It was really kind of you.	你人真好。
⓱	It was the most precious gift I've ever received.	这是我收到的最珍贵的礼物。

⑱ The earrings you gave me are absolutely beautiful.　你送给我的耳环真是太漂亮了。

⑲ You've been so supportive from the start.　你从一开始就非常支持我。

⑳ I appreciate your hard work.　我很感激你的辛苦工作。

㉑ I truly appreciate it.　我真地很感激。

㉒ I really can't thank you enough.　我实在对你感谢不尽。

㉓ I can't express my gratitude enough.　我怎么表达感激之情也不过分。

㉔ I couldn't have done it without your help.　没有你的帮助，我是无法完成的。

㉕ I wouldn't have been able to do it without your help.　没有你的帮助，我是做不来的。

㉖ Thank you for the wonderful dinner last night.　谢谢你昨晚丰盛的晚宴。

㉗ I appreciate your kindness and hospitality.　谢谢你的友好和热情款待。

㉘ We enjoyed meeting with you and your family.　很高兴见到你和你的家人。

㉙ You really cheered me up last night.　昨晚我真的很高兴。

㉚ I'd like to have you over to our place soon, too.　我也希望你不久能到我们这儿来。

㉛ I'll cherish your gift for years to come.　我会永远珍惜你的礼物。

㉜ I thank you from the bottom of my heart.　我衷心地感谢你。

信例1（生活类）

Dear Jen,

Thanks so much for the lovely dinner on Friday night. You're really a wonderful chef! If was so nice to see you and Bob again, and your new cat, too. Shane and I are going on a trip next week, but we'd like to invite you over to our place when we get back.

With love,

Carol

非常感谢周五愉快的晚餐，你真是个很棒的厨师。如果能看到你和鲍勃还有你新养的猫，那就太好了。我和谢恩下周要去旅行，回来后一定要请你们到我们这儿来。

Dear Mr. Bennett,

We received your gift basket this morning—it was very thoughtful of you! The Swiss chocolate is especially delicious. It's always a pleasure to provide our accounting services to you, and we're honored to have you as both our client and friend. We wish you and your business every success in the new year.

Sincerely,

Joanne Thompson

今天早晨我们收到了你的礼物，你真是太体贴了！瑞士巧克力格外好吃。能够为你提供会计服务我们感到很高兴，同时我们也很荣幸你能够成为我们的客户和朋友。祝你在新的一年里生意兴隆、蒸蒸日上。

4 祝愿和祝贺 Expressing good wishes and congratulations

生日祝福 *Birthday wishes*

❶ Happy birthday!   生日快乐！

❷ I hope you have a happy birthday!   祝你生日快乐！

❸ We all wish you a very happy birthday.   我们都祝福你过一个快乐的生日。

❹ Congratulations on your 20th/30th/40th birthday!   祝贺你的 20 岁/30 岁/40 岁生日。

❺ May your birthday be filled with joy and happiness.   祝你的生日充满愉悦与快乐。

❻ I wish I could be there to celebrate your birthday with you.   我真希望能和你一起庆祝你的生日。

❼ We send you our best wishes for a happy birthday.   寄予我们最美好的祝愿，祝你生日快乐。

节日祝福 *Holiday wishes*

❶ Happy Holidays!   节日快乐！

❷ Happy New Year!   新年快乐！

❸ Merry Christmas!   圣诞快乐！

❹ Happy Hanukkah!   光明节快乐！

❺ Happy Easter!   复活节快乐！

❻ Happy Valentine's Day!   情人节快乐！

❼ Happy Thanksgiving!   感恩节快乐！

❽ Happy Halloween!   万圣节快乐！

⑨ I wish you a Merry Christmas and a Happy New Year!　祝你圣诞快乐、新年快乐！

⑩ I wish you health and happiness in the coming year!　祝你明年身体健康、生活愉快！

⑪ I hope you have a wonderful holiday season!　祝你假期过得愉快！

⑫ I would like to wish you all the best for a wonderful holiday season.　祝你假期快乐，一切顺利。

⑬ We send you our very best wishes for the holidays.　我们寄去最诚挚的祝福，祝您假期愉快。

⑭ We would like to wish you and your family a happy holiday season.　我们祝您和您的家人假期愉快。

⑮ I look forward to seeing you at the New Year's Eve party.　期盼着在新年晚会上见到你。

⑯ We're thinking of you and your family and wish you could be here with us.　我们一直很想念你和你的家人，真希望你能跟我们在一起。

⑰ We love you and miss you very much.　我们很爱你，也非常想念你。

⑱ May all the joys of Christmas be yours!　祝圣诞节愉快！

⑲ May your new year be filled with health and happiness.　祝您在新的一年里身体健康、生活愉快。

⑳ May the coming year bring you happiness, health and prosperity.　祝您在新的一年快乐、健康、兴旺。

㉑ I hope that your holiday season is filled with joy and laughter.　祝你假期快乐欢愉。

恭贺入学 *Congratulations on school acceptances*

❶ Congratulations on your acceptance to law/medical school!　祝贺你考入法学院/医学院。

❷ I would like to congratulate you on your acceptance to graduate school!　祝贺你考上了研究生。

❸ I just heard that you were accepted to the University of Cambridge.　我刚刚听说你被剑桥大学录取了。

❹ I would like to express my warmest/sincerest congratulations.　我要表达我最诚挚的祝贺。

⑤ I know that this has been your dream for so long.　我知道这一直是你多年的梦想。

⑥ This is the result of all your hard work and dedication over the years.　这是你多年辛苦工作的结果。

⑦ We are all so proud of you.　我们真为你骄傲。

⑧ I wish you all the best in your studies.　祝你学业有成。

⑨ I heard that your son/daughter received a full scholarship to Cornell University.　我听说你的儿子/女儿拿到了康奈尔大学的全额奖学金。

⑩ You must be so proud of him/her.　你一定很为他/她骄傲。

恭贺新婚 *Congratulating newlyweds*

❶ Congratulations on your engagement/marriage/wedding!　祝你们新婚快乐!

❷ You have our best wishes for a lifetime of love and happiness together.　祝你们相亲相爱、幸福快乐。

❸ I'm looking forward to attending your wedding in June.　期盼着6月份参加你们的婚礼。

❹ May you have a blessed and joyful life together!　祝你们在一起幸福快乐。

❺ The two of you are a match made in heaven.　你们俩是天生的一对。

❻ Please accept my heartiest congratulations on your son's/daughter's marriage.　对你儿子/女儿的婚姻表示我最衷心的祝贺。

❼ Please also express our best wishes to the rest of your family.　请代我向你家人问好。

❽ I wish the two of you a happy and healthy life together!　祝你们新婚快乐、白头偕老。

恭贺升迁 *Congratulations on promotions*

❶ Congratulations on your promotion!　祝贺你提职!

❷ Congratulations on your promotion to the position of manager/vice-president/president!　祝贺你提升为经理/副主席/主席!

❸ You certainly/definitely deserve it!　这绝对是你应该得到的!

❹ You've worked so hard these past years and you deserve it.　过去这几年你工作得太辛苦了，这是你应得的。

⑤ You're moving up in the world! 　　　你在步步高升啊！

⑥ Please accept our best wishes for every 　请接受我们最良好的祝愿，祝你在新的
success in your new position. 　　　　岗位上获得成功。

⑦ I wish you every success in your new 　祝你在新的岗位上取得成功。
position.

⑧ I was glad to learn of your appointment 　得知你被任命为地区经理，我很高兴。
as regional manager.

⑨ I was extremely pleased to learn of your 　听说你高升了，我非常高兴。
promotion.

祝愿 *Expressing good wishes*

❶ I wish you a safe/pleasant journey. 　　祝你一路平安/旅途愉快。

❷ I'm sure that you'll have a great/ 　　祝你旅行愉快。
wonderful/fantastic trip.

❸ I hope you have a great/super/fantastic 　祝你玩儿得高兴。
time.

❹ Good luck in your new endeavors. 　　　祝你好运。

❺ Best wishes for the holidays. 　　　　祝你假期快乐。

❻ May all your dreams come true! 　　　祝你梦想成真！

❼ Please remember me to your family/ 　请代我向你的家人/父母/妈妈/爸爸
parents/mother/father. 　　　　　　问好。

❽ Please give my best wishes to everyone. 　请代我向大家致意。

❾ Please say hi to everyone for me. 　　代我向大家问好。

信例 1（生活类）

Dear Paul,

Congratulations on your acceptance to medical school at Johns Hopkins University! I know how hard you've been studying for the past three years. This is the culmination of all your efforts—you deserve it. Give me a shout when you're free and I'll take you out for a drink to celebrate.

See you soon,

Marianne

祝贺你考入了约翰·霍普金斯大学医学院！我知道你在过去的 3 年里有多刻苦学习，这是你努力的结果，你应得的。你什么时候有时间叫我，我们出去喝点儿庆祝一下。

Dear Ms. Liu,

I'd like to offer my heartfelt congratulations to you on your appointment as Asia-Pacific Marketing Director. You've shown tremendous leadership and ingenuity, so your promotion comes as no surprise to me. Everyone at the office will miss you....

Make sure you write to us once you get settled in Hong Kong.

Best regards,

Wang Hong

衷心的祝贺你成为亚太地区销售部主管。对你的提升我一点儿都不觉得惊奇，因为你早就展现出了非凡的领导才能和智慧。办公室的每一个人都会想你的……你在香港一安顿下来就要给我们写信呀。

5 道歉 Apologies

道歉 *Making an apology*

❶ I'm sorry to have troubled/inconvenienced you.   抱歉给您添麻烦了。

❷ I'm sorry that I didn't get back to you sooner/earlier.   抱歉没能快点儿/早点儿回来。

❸ I'm sorry for making such a careless mistake.   我做事粗心大意的，真不好意思。

❹ I'm very sorry for having kept you waiting so long.   不好意思让你等了这么长时间。

❺ I'm really sorry for having made such a thoughtless comment.   很抱歉我做出这样轻率的评论。

❻ Sorry for the long delay in replying to your e-mail.   很抱歉耽搁这么长时间才给您回邮件。

❼ Sorry for not writing to you sooner/earlier.   不好意思没有尽快/早点儿给您写信。

❽ I apologize for having caused you so much trouble.   很抱歉给您带来这么多麻烦。

❾ I would like to apologize for having taken so much of your time.   很抱歉占用了您这么多时间。

⑩ Please forgive me for my late reply/ response.

这么晚才给您回复，请原谅。

⑪ Please forgive me.

请原谅。

表示原谅 *Expressing forgiveness*

❶ Of course I forgive you.

我当然原谅你了。

❷ I'm willing to forgive you.

我会原谅你的。

❸ Let's put this incident in the past and move on.

让这事过去吧，我们得往前看。

❹ After all, it's not a big deal in the grand scheme of things.

毕竟对这么大个项目来说，这也不是什么大不了的事。

❺ I think that I'm partly to blame, too.

我想我也有一部分责任。

❻ You're not the one to blame.

不该责备你。

❼ You're not the only one to blame.

责任不该由你一个人承担。

❽ Please don't blame yourself.

别责备自己了。

❾ It isn't/wasn't completely your fault.

这不完全是你的错。

⑩ It isn't/wasn't your fault.

这不是你的错。

信例1（生活类）

Hi Sally,

I'm sorry I wasn't able to make it to your party last night. My boss called late in the afternoon and asked me to help finish an urgent project. I tried calling you but wasn't able to get through. Anyway, I hope everyone had a great time. Please accept my sincere apologies.

Yours,

William

很抱歉昨晚没能参加你们的聚会。我老板下午很晚给我打了个电话，让我帮他完成一个紧急项目。我给你打电话，但没能接通。不管怎么样，我希望你们玩儿得都很开心。请接受我诚挚的道歉。

Dear Neil,

Sorry for the delay in replying to your e-mail. I looked over your suggestions, and I think most of them are feasible. If you don't mind, I'll forward a copy directly to the head of the budget committee. He might contact you if he has any questions. Keep up the impressive work.

Regards,

Ted Stein

很抱歉这么晚才给你写回信。你的建议我看了，我觉得大部分都是可行的。如果你不介意，我直接给预算委员会的领导转发一份。如果他有问题可能会与你联系。你工作得很出色，继续努力！

⑥ 表示慰问 Expressing condolences

❶ I share your pain/sorrow/sadness.   我和你一样痛苦/难过/悲伤。

❷ You must be feeling terrible/awful right now.   你现在一定感到悲伤/难过。

❸ I'm truly/deeply/extremely sorry to hear that.   听到这个消息我真是非常难过。

❹ I can relate to how you are feeling.   我能体会你的感受。

❺ Please accept my deepest sympathy.   请接受我最深切的同情。

❻ Please accept my sincere condolences.   请接受我最真诚的哀悼。

❼ Take it easy and get plenty of rest.   放松一下，好好休息休息。

❽ I hope you feel better soon.   希望你尽快好起来。

❾ I wish you a speedy/quick recovery.   希望你能迅速康复。

❿ I'm so sorry to hear of your mother's/father's death.   听说你妈妈/爸爸去世了，我很难过。

⓫ We are saddened to learn that your mother/father has passed away.   听说你妈妈/爸爸去世了，我们很伤心。

⓬ Please accept my condolences on the death of your mother/father.   请接受我对你母亲/父亲的去世表示哀悼。

⓭ I know how hard it is to lose a parent.   我知道失去父母让人很难过。

⓮ If you need anything at all, please just let me know.   如果你需要任何帮助，尽管告诉我。

⓯ I'm so/very sorry to hear about your car accident.   听说你出了车祸，我很难过。

⑯ I was really/greatly shocked to hear about your accident.

听说你出了事故，太令我震惊了。

⑰ I just heard from Andrew that you caught the flu.

我刚从安德鲁那听说你感冒了。

⑱ I hope you're doing better now and keeping your spirits up.

我希望你好起来，振作起来。

⑲ I'm so relieved to hear that you're out of the hospital and back with your family.

听说你已经出院和家人回家了，我就放心了。

⑳ All you need to focus on right now is relaxing and getting better.

你现在要做的就是放松并好起来。

㉑ Please let me know if there's anything I can do for you and your family.

如果有什么我能为你和你家人做的，尽管告诉我。

㉒ Please let us know if there's anything we can do for you.

如果有什么我们能帮你做的，就告诉我们。

㉓ If there is anything you need, please let me know.

如果你需要什么就告诉我。

㉔ I'm sorry to learn that your new bicycle was stolen.

得知你的自行车被偷了，我很难过。

㉕ I'm really sorry about your wallet being stolen.

你的钱包丢了，我真的为你难过。

㉖ I am so sorry to hear about your dog/cat passing away.

听说你的狗/猫死了，我很难过。

㉗ We are saddened to learn that Beth has gone to heaven.

得知贝丝过世，我们很伤心。

㉘ You have my heartfelt/deepest sympathy.

我对你深表同情。

信例1（生活类）

Dear Betsy,

I'm really sorry to hear about your car accident. I know how upset you must be, especially with it being a new car. But the important thing is that no one was injured. You're the most careful driver I know, so don't blame yourself. Please let me know if there's anything I can do for you.

Love,

Monica

听说你出了车祸，我很难过。我知道你现在一定很伤心，尤其这是一辆新车。但重要的是没人受伤。我知道你开车一向很谨慎，别太责怪自己了。如果有什么需要我帮助的尽管说。

Dear Jeff,

I just heard about your father's passing away, and I want you to know how deeply sorry I am for your loss. If there's anything I can help you with, either at the office or otherwise, please let me know. Grieving takes time, so try to take things easy for a while.

Yours,

Thomas

我刚刚听说你父亲过世了，我真为你难过。如果有什么需要我帮助，不管是工作上的，还是其他方面的，一定要告诉我。时间会淡漠痛苦，别太难过了，慢慢会好起来的。

7 约定时间/计划 Arranging time and making plans

询问 Inquiring about plans

❶ What time should we arrange to meet? 我们应该安排什么时间见面？

❷ When would be a good time for us to meet? 我们什么时间见面合适？

❸ What time do you think we should meet? 你觉得我们该什么时候见面？

❹ Shall we meet this evening at 6:00 then? 我们今晚 6 点见面怎么样？

❺ When are you expecting to arrive? 你期望什么时候到？

❻ When and where should I pick you up? 我什么时间到哪儿接你？

❼ How about we meet at 9:00 am tomorrow at the coffee shop? 明天上午 9 点在咖啡厅见怎么样？

❽ Would 6:00 this evening work for you? 今晚 6 点对你合适吗？

❾ Would either Saturday or Sunday be convenient for you? 你周六方便还是周日方便？

❿ Shall we meet at 7:30 at the entrance to the cinema? 我们 7 点半在电影院门口见面怎么样？

⓫ If it's convenient for you, I'll swing by your place around 5:00. 如果你方便的话，我 5 点左右到你那。

⓬ I'll pick you up at the hotel at 11:00, okay? 我 11 点到宾馆接你，好吗？

⑬ Don't forget to let me know your flight schedule. 别忘了告诉我你的飞机航班?

⑭ I would be glad to pick you up at the train station. 我很高兴到火车站接你。

⑮ When does your train arrive at Beijing Railway Station? 你的火车几点到北京站?

⑯ What's your departure/arrival time? 你什么时候离开/到达?

⑰ Let me know what time you're expecting to arrive. 告诉我你什么时候到?

⑱ I'd like to invite you to my place for dinner on Wednesday. 我想邀请你周三到我这儿吃晚餐。

⑲ I'll be here all week, so let me know when you have time to meet. 我整个一周都在这儿,你什么时候有时间见面告诉我。

⑳ I have tickets to a basketball game tomorrow afternoon at 1:30. 我有明天下午一点半篮球比赛的票。

㉑ How about dinner Thursday or Friday evening? 周四或周五一起共进晚餐怎么样?

㉒ How long are you planning to stay? 你打算待多长时间?

㉓ Which hotel are you staying at? 您住在哪个宾馆?

㉔ What time do you need to get to the airport on Tuesday? 您周二需要几点到机场?

㉕ If we leave at 3:00, we'll definitely get there on time. 如果我们 3 点出发的话,一定能准时到达。

㉖ Could we meet at 2:00 instead of 1:30? 我们别一点半见了,两点见面怎么样?

应答 *Replying*

❶ I'm leaving for Brazil next Thursday. 我下周四动身前往巴西。

❷ I'll be on a business trip in Bangkok from July 12 to 15. 我 7 月 12 日到 15 日去曼谷出差。

❸ I'll be returning to China by the end of the month. 我这个月底回国。

❹ I'll call/e-mail/contact you as soon as I'm back. 我一回来就给你打电话/发邮件/和你联系。

❺ My flight arrives on the morning of March 3. 我的飞机 3 月 3 日早晨到。

⑥ I'll have a one-week holiday starting next Monday.   从下周一开始我有一周的假期。

⑦ I'll phone you later this evening to confirm.   我今晚晚些时候给你打电话确认。

⑧ 10:00 tomorrow morning would be perfect.   明早 10 点非常合适。

⑨ I'll be arriving at Beijing Railway Station at 10:30 am.   我上午 10 点半到北京火车站。

⑩ I'm so glad to hear that you're coming to Dalian.   得知你要来大连我很高兴。

⑪ I'll let you know my schedule/itinerary as soon as it's confirmed.   我的日程安排一确定就告诉你。

⑫ That sounds great. I'll see you bright and early Saturday morning.   听起来不错。周六一大清早我去见你。

⑬ Sure, a round of golf on Saturday morning sounds great.   当然，周六早晨打场高尔夫太好了。

⑭ I look forward to seeing you tomorrow!   我期待明天见到你。

⑮ I'm so sorry that I won't be able to see you this weekend.   很抱歉这周末我不能见你了。

⑯ We'll find another time to get together soon.   我们再找个时间聚聚。

⑰ I'll call you before I leave to pick you up.   我去接你之前给你电话。

⑱ I'll see you Saturday afternoon then.   周六下午我去见你。

信例 1（生活类）

Hi, Mary,

It's hard to believe that the winter holiday is almost over. Have you booked your return flight yet? Let me know the flight number, and the date and time you'll be coming in. I can arrange to pick you up at the airport. Hope you're enjoying your last few days in Melbourne. See you soon!

Best regards,

Clarence

真不敢相信寒假就要结束了。你已经订好回去的机票了吗？到时告诉我航班号、日期和你到达的具体时间，我好安排去机场接你。祝你在墨尔本的最后几天玩儿得愉快！到时候见。

信例2（商务类）

Dear Roger,

I'm going to be in Vancouver next month on a business trip. If you're not too busy, let's find a time to get together. The exact date isn't confirmed yet, but I'll probably be flying in on the 3rd or 4th and staying for about two weeks. Please let me know your schedule.

Kind regards,

Terrence

我下个月要去温哥华出差。如果你不太忙的话，我们可以找个时间聚聚。我的具体时间还没定，不过很可能是3号或者4号到，在那待两个星期。把你的时间表告诉我吧。

8 询问联系方式 Asking for contact information

❶ Do you know Carl's new address? | 你知道卡尔的新地址吗？

❷ Would you mind giving me Denise's e-mail address? | 你介意把丹尼斯的电子邮箱地址给我吗？

❸ Please let me know how I can reach him. | 请告诉我怎么能找到他。

❹ What's the best/easiest way to reach her? | 怎么能以最快速度找到她？

❺ Do you have Erica's phone number? | 你有埃里卡的电话号码吗？

❻ I need to contact her as soon as possible. | 我需要尽快和她联系。

❼ There's something I would like to discuss with her. | 我有事要和她商量。

❽ I've been trying to reach Fred for a long time, but to no avail. | 我一直在找弗雷德，找了好长时间也没找到。

❾ Have you heard from him lately? | 你最近收到他的信了吗？

❿ If you see George this weekend, please ask him to call me. | 这周末如果你看见乔治的话，请让他给我打电话。

⓫ I heard you moved to a new house/condo/apartment. | 我听说你搬进新房子/新公寓了。

⓬ Please let me know your address so I can return those books you lent me. | 请告诉我你的地址，我好把你借给我的那些书还给你。

⓭ I tried calling you yesterday, but I think I might have the wrong number. | 我昨天试图给你打电话，但我可能把号码记错了。

⓮ I want to send you a postcard, so please let me know your address.

我想给你寄名信片，请把你的地址告诉我。

⓯ Could you let me know your new address when you have a chance?

什么时候有机会，能把你的新地址告诉我吗？

⓰ I'd like to get in touch with Harriet but I can't find her e-mail address.

我想跟哈丽特联系，可是我找不到她的电子邮箱地址了。

⓱ Do you have her contact information?

你有她的联系方式吗？

⓲ I tried sending Ivan an e-mail, but it was bounced back for some reason.

我给伊凡发了封邮件，可不知道什么原因给退回来了。

⓳ Do you know if he switched to a new e-mail address?

你知道他是不是换新电子邮箱地址了？

信例1（生活类）

Hi Ralph,

How've you been recently? I heard from Alex that you moved to a condo downtown last week. Could you let me know your new phone number when you get a chance? There's something I'd like to discuss with you. Maybe we could meet up once you get settled in your new place.

Regards,

Angela

最近怎么样？我从亚历克斯那听说你上周搬到市区公寓大楼了。有机会的话能告诉我你的新电话号码吗？我有事想与你商量。可能的话你在新地方安顿下来后我们见一面。

信例2（商务类）

Dear Leah,

I understand that Dave Anderson, one of the summer interns, doesn't have any work assigned to him at the moment. If you don't mind, I'd like to ask him to help out with copyediting in the editorial department. Please let me know his extension and e-mail address, and I'll contact him directly this afternoon.

Many thanks,

Rick

我知道一个叫戴夫·安德森的暑期实习生，目前没有分配到任何工作。如果你不介意的话，我想让他到编辑部帮忙校对。请告诉我他的分机号和邮箱，今天下午我会直接和他联系。

9 告知消息 Conveying news

好消息　*Good news*

❶ I've got some great/wonderful news to tell you. 　我有好消息要告诉你。

❷ I can't believe how lucky I was. 　我不敢相信我这么幸运。

❸ Guess what! I finally got my driver's license! 　你猜怎么着，我终于拿到了驾照。

❹ I'm starting the new job on Monday! 　我周一就要开始新的工作了。

❺ The tech stock I bought last month has more than doubled! 　我上个月买的科技股已经翻两番了。

❻ I found the perfect Valentine's Day gift for him/her! 　我给他/她买到了精美的情人节礼物。

❼ My son/daughter is getting married! 　我儿子/女儿要结婚了。

坏消息　*Bad news*

❶ I have some unfortunate news. 　我有个不幸的消息。

❷ I'm afraid I have some bad news. 　恐怕我有不好的消息。

❸ I had a minor car accident this morning. 　今天早上我出了个小车祸。

❹ I had an awful day today. 　今天太糟糕了。

❺ My day went from bad to worse. 　每况愈下。

❻ Our house was broken into last night. 　我们家昨晚被盗了。

❼ I never thought this would happen to me. 　我从未想过这种事情会发生在我身上。

❽ I was stuck in traffic all afternoon. 　我被堵在路上，堵了整整一下午。

❾ My flight was delayed for over five hours. 　我的飞机晚点了5个多小时。

❿ Jane and Kevin are getting a divorce. 　简和凯文正在闹离婚。

⓫ Louise didn't get the job offer. 　路易斯没有得到这份工作。

⓬ My dog/cat passed away yesterday. 　我的狗/猫昨天死了。

⓭ My car was stolen. 　我的车被偷了。

Hi Doug,

I've been feeling really sick the whole week, so I finally went to see the doctor this morning. He said I have mononucleosis. I don't mind missing a few classes ... but I also have two term papers due next Friday, and I don't have the energy to write them. What do you think I should do?

Michelle

这个星期我一直觉得不舒服，今天早上我到底去看了医生。大夫说我得了单核细胞增多症。我不在乎落下几节课，但是下周五我有两个学期论文该交了，我没有精力写。你认为我该怎么办呢？

Dear Betty,

I have some good news to share with you. The client was pleased with the new ad layout and decided to renew their contract with us. I know you haven't been with our company very long, but you've been doing excellent work. Your contributions on this project made a significant difference.

Best regards,

Bill Parker

我有好消息告诉你。客户非常满意这个新的广告设计，决定要跟我们续签合同。我知道你来公司时间不长，但你的工作一直非常出色。你对这个项目的贡献很大，使整个项目大有起色。

第二部分　提出想法
Proposing Ideas

⑩ 邀请 Invitations

提出邀请 Offering an invitation

❶ Do you want to get together for coffee this weekend?

这周末你想一起去喝咖啡吗？

❷ How about catching a movie tomorrow night?

明天晚上看电影怎么样？

❸ Mark and I would like to invite you to our place on Saturday evening.

马克和我想邀请你周六晚上来我们家。

❹ Would you be up for playing tennis tomorrow morning?

明天一早你们起来打网球吗？

❺ I'm having a house warming party Friday night and I hope you can come.

周五晚上我要在家开个晚会，希望你能来。

❻ Do you want to go dancing this weekend?

这周末你想去跳舞吗？

❼ I'd really like to see you while you're in town.

你们在市里时，我真得很想去看你们。

❽ Perhaps we could get together for lunch one day this week.

这周哪天可能的话我们可以一起吃顿午餐。

❾ Would you be interested in taking a yoga class with me?

你想跟我一起去上瑜伽课吗？

❿ Let's go shopping together this weekend, okay?

这周末我们一起逛街，好吗？

⓫ Just let me know if you're interested.

请告知我你是否感兴趣。

⓬ It would be really nice to see you again.

又看见你真是太好了。

⓭ Let me know if you're available so I can make the arrangements.

如果您有时间请告诉我，我好作安排。

⓮ We'd like to invite you to spend the weekend at our cottage.

我们想邀请你来我们的别墅度周末。

⓯ Please let me know as soon as possible if you can come.

请尽快告诉我你是否能来。

接受邀请 *Accepting an invitation*

❶ Thanks for the invitation!   感谢您的邀请。

❷ Thanks for asking me!   多谢问我。

❸ I'd love to go to the museum with you this weekend.   很高兴周末和你一起去博物馆。

❹ Golf tomorrow morning sounds great.   明天早上打高尔夫听起来好极了。

❺ Lunch on Sunday would be really nice.   周日一起吃午餐太好了。

❻ I'm not too familiar with the downtown area, so I'll let you pick the restaurant.   我不是很熟悉这个街区，所以我想让你来选餐馆。

❼ Can I bring anything to the party?   我要带什么东西到晚会吗？

❽ I'll bring a bottle of wine.   我会带瓶红酒。

❾ I'm really looking forward to seeing your new place.   我很想看看你的新住所。

❿ Just let me know what time I should come over.   请告知我应该什么时候过来。

⓫ I'm kind of busy on Saturday, but I should be free all day on Sunday.   周六我有点儿忙，但我周日一整天都有时间。

⓬ Check your schedule and let me know if that works for you.   查看一下你的日程表然后告诉我这个时间对你是否合适。

⓭ It'll be great to see you again!   又能见到你太好了。

拒绝邀请 *Declining an invitation*

❶ Unfortunately, I have some prior engagements this weekend.   真可惜，我这周末已经事先有安排了。

❷ Thanks for asking me, but I'm going to be in India at that time.   非常感谢您问我，但是可惜那时我在印度呢。

❸ I'll call you when I get back and hopefully we can get together then.   我回来给你打电话，希望我们那时能聚一聚。

❹ I'd really like to come, but I have some other plans.   我真是非常想来，可是我已经有别的安排了。

❺ I really wish I could go with you, but I promised to help my friend move on Saturday.   我真希望能跟你一起去，但是我已答应朋友周六去帮他搬家了。

❻ If you're free, maybe we could get together sometime next week instead.   如果你有时间，我们可以改在下周什么时间聚一聚。

❼ Unfortunately, I have to work overtime tomorrow night.   不巧的是，明天晚上我得加班。

❽ I'll have a lot more time after I finish this translation project.   我完成这个翻译项目之后就会有更多的时间了。

⑨ This week is pretty hectic, but I'm sure we can find another time to meet soon.

这周实在是太忙了，我相信很快我们可以另找个时间见面。

⑩ I would love to attend, but my relatives are coming in from out of town that day.

我很想参加，但是我的亲戚那天从外地过来。

⑪ I'm going out to dinner for my dad's birthday that night.

我打算在我爸爸生日的那天晚上出去吃。

⑫ I should have a lot more time as soon as I finish writing my thesis.

我一完成论文就会有很多时间了。

⑬ We'll find another time to get together soon though.

我们另找个时间聚一聚。

⑭ Thanks for the invitation all the same.

仍然感谢您的邀请。

⑮ Thanks for inviting me anyway.

不管怎样要感谢您邀请我。

信例 1（生活类）

Hey Laura,
Do you have any plans for the long weekend? I was talking to Mia today, and she suggested the three of us go to Florida and hit the beach! I think it would be a good time. Anyway, give me a call tonight and let me know what you think.
Talk to you soon,
Beatrice

这个长周末你有什么安排吗？今天我跟米亚聊天，她建议我们三个去佛罗里达沙滩。我觉得会玩儿得很开心。不管怎么样，晚上给我打个电话，说说你的想法。

信例 2（商务类）

Dear Leo,
Golf on Saturday morning sounds great. I just got a new set of clubs last week, so this will give me a chance to break them in. How about meeting at the usual place at 9:00? If you're not doing anything afterwards, let's have lunch together after our game.
See you Saturday,
Gabriel

周六早晨去打高尔夫球好极了。上周我刚买了一副新球杆，这可有机会练一练了。9点钟老地方见怎么样？如果你没什么事情的话我们打完球一起吃午饭。

11 提醒 Reminders

❶ Don't forget to book the train tickets a few days in advance.

别忘了提前几天订火车票。

❷ Remember to devote enough time to your studies.

记着要投入足够的时间学习。

❸ Even though you're busy at work, it's important that you get enough rest.

尽管你工作很忙，但充足的休息也很重要。

❹ You should get to the airport at least two hours prior to departure.

你应该在飞机起飞前两个小时到机场。

❺ Please make sure you arrive on time.

要保证准时到。

❻ Remember to listen to your doctor's advice.

记着要听医生的建议。

❼ Remember to bring your student card to the examination.

一定要带学生卡去考试。

❽ Please remember to finish the proposal by Friday.

请记住周五前要完成提案。

❾ I'd like to remind you that yesterday's meeting was rescheduled to 4:00 today.

我想提醒你昨天的会议改到今天 4 点了。

❿ I know how busy you are, so I just wanted to make sure you remembered.

我知道你非常忙，所以我就想提醒你一下。

⓫ You'll remember to keep your promise, right?

你会记得你的承诺，是吧？

⓬ You haven't forgotten about our lunch tomorrow, have you?

别忘了我们明天中午吃午餐。

信例 1（生活类）

Dear Students,

I would like to remind you that there will be no tutorial this week. If you have any questions, please send me an e-mail or drop by during my regular office hours. Also, remember that next week's final will be cumulative, so you'll need to review last term's material. Good luck to you all.

Sincerely,

Tim Bergman

我想提醒大家本周没有辅导课，如果你们有什么问题，可以给我发邮件或者在办公时间到办公室找我。还有我们下周期末考试是大考，所以你们需要复习上学期的所有内容。祝大家好运。

信例2（商务类）

Dear Rob,

I was wondering whether you've had a chance to revise the presentation slides yet. The meeting is in two days, and I'd like to look over the revised version by tomorrow at the latest. If you're tied up with other work, I can ask Clarence to help out. Please let me know soon though.

Cordially,

Gary

我想知道演讲幻灯片有没有改好。会议还有两天就举行了，我想明天再最后看看修改版。如果你有其他工作太忙的话，我可以让克拉伦斯帮帮忙。不管怎么样，尽快通知我。

12 请求帮助 Requesting help

❶ I was wondering if you could do me a favor.

我想知道您是否能帮助我。

❷ Could you take a look at my website and give me some suggestions?

您能看看我的网站，给我些建议吗？

❸ Do you think you could give me a hand with the assignment?

我的论文您能帮我个忙吗？

❹ Do you think I could borrow your car on Saturday night?

我周六晚上能借一下您的车吗？

❺ Would you mind proofreading my essay for me?

你介意帮我校对论文吗？

❻ Would you mind picking up my mail while I'm away?

你介意我不在的时候帮我取信吗？

❼ Would you have time to help me move this weekend?

您这周末有时间帮我搬家吗？

❽ Please ask Nancy to call me when she has a chance.

请让南希有机会给我打电话。

❾ Do you think you could help me fix my computer?

你能帮我修修电脑吗？

❿ I'd appreciate it if you could pick me up at the train station tomorrow.

如果您明天能在火车站接我，我将十分感激。

⓫ If you're seeing Oliver tomorrow, could you return his book for me?

如果明天你能看见奥利弗的话，能帮我把书还给他吗？

⑫ We're looking for volunteers to help out during the holiday season. 　我们正在找志愿者假期来帮忙。

⑬ I would greatly appreciate it if you could assist me. 　如果您能帮助我，我将不胜感激。

⑭ I would really appreciate your help. 　我真的很感激您的帮助。

⑮ If you're too busy, I would understand. 　如果你很忙，我会理解的。

表示不能帮助 Expressing inability to help

❶ I'd really like to give you a hand, but I'm going to be away for the holidays. 　我真的很愿意帮助你，但是我假期要外出。

❷ I wish that I could help, but I've got so many things to do tomorrow. 　我真希望我能帮助你，但是我明天有很多事情要做。

❸ Unfortunately, I just lent that book to someone else yesterday. 　不好意思，我昨天刚刚把这本书借给别人了。

❹ I have to meet a client on Saturday morning, so I'm afraid I won't be able to pick you up. 　我周六早晨必须去见客户，所以恐怕我不能去接你了。

❺ If Thursday wouldn't be too late, I would probably be able to help you then. 　如果周四不晚的话，我到时去帮你。

信例1（生活类）

Hi Lisa,

As you know, I'll be studying in France next semester. I want to find a part-time job while I'm over there … but right now I only have a résumé in English. Would you mind helping me translate it into French? I'm not leaving till January, so there's still plenty of time. I'd really appreciate it.

Kindest regards,

Stephen

你知道我下学期要到法国学习。我想到时在那找份兼职。可是现在我只有用英文写的简历，你能帮我翻译成法语吗？我到一月份才走，时间比较充裕。真是太感谢你了。

Dear Ed,

I woke up this morning with a splitting headache, so I didn't come to work today. Could you do me a favor? There's an envelope on my desk which I forgot to send out yesterday. It's sealed and addressed—it just needs postage. I would appreciate it if you could give me a hand.

Thanks,

Samuel

我今早醒来头疼得好像要裂开一样，所以今天不能去上班了。我想请你帮个忙，我桌子上有个信封，昨天我忘了寄了。信封已经封口了，地址也写好了，就差邮寄了。如果你能帮我邮寄出去，我会特别感激。

13 提供帮助 Offering help

❶ Let me know if I can help you finish the report.

如果需要我帮你完成报告的话就告诉我。

❷ If you're interested, I could get you a free ticket to the concert.

如果你感兴趣，我可以给你一张免费的票去听音乐会。

❸ I'll pick up some snacks and drinks for the party, okay?

我会买点儿快餐和饮料去参加晚会，好吗？

❹ Would you like me to book your hotel reservations?

你需要我帮你预订宾馆的房间吗？

❺ Do you need any help with your assignment?

你需要我帮你完成任务吗？

Hi Richard,

How's it going? I know you've been stressing out over your psych class recently. I actually did pretty well in that course last year, and I'd be glad to help you get ready for the final. My schedule is pretty light this week, too … so just drop me a line if you're interested.

Best wishes,

Sylvia

最近怎么样？我知道你最近心理学课程的压力很大。去年我这门课学得很好，我很愿意帮助你准备期末考试。这周我没什么事，如果你有意的话就写信告诉我。

Hi Frank,

Are you still trying to get tickets for this weekend's basketball playoffs? As it happens, I know someone with a pair of seats who can't go anymore. If you're interested, I could probably get the tickets at a good price. But try to let me know soon, before he sells them to someone else.

Best regards,

Bernard

你是在买这个周末篮球决赛的门票吗？如果真是这样的话，我知道有人有两张票但是他们去不了了。如果你有兴趣的话，我可能会以优惠的价格拿到票。但是你一定要在他们把票卖出去之前尽快告诉我。

14 建议 Suggestions

请求指点/征求建议 *Asking for guidance or suggestions*

❶ I'm not sure how to resolve this issue.　我不知道怎样解决这个问题。

❷ How should I solve this problem?　我应该怎样解决这个问题呢？

❸ I can't figure out what to do.　我不知道怎么做？

❹ What do you suggest I do?　你建议我做什么呢？

❺ Could you give me some tips?　你能给我些建议吗？

❻ What would you do if you were me?　如果你是我，你会怎么做？

❼ I'm not quite sure how to handle this situation.　我不确定怎么解决这种情况。

❽ I was wondering if you could offer me some advice.　我想知道你是否能给我提供一些建议。

❾ I would appreciate any of your suggestions/recommendations.　您的任何建议/意见，我都十分感激。

❿ Where do you think Patrick and I should go for our vacation?　你觉得我和帕特里克应该去哪度假呢？

⓫ What do you think I should get for her birthday present?　你觉得我应该送给她什么作为生日礼物呢？

⓬ I can't decide whether I should study overseas or not.　我还没决定是否要去海外学习。

⓭ I can't figure out which kind of car to buy.　我不知道要买哪种车？

⑭ Do you think it would be better for me to buy or lease? 　你觉得我是买好还是租好呢？

⑮ Do you think I should talk to my boss about this matter? 　你认为我应该和老板谈谈这个事情吗？

⑯ What brand of computer do you think I should buy? 　你认为我应该买什么牌子的电脑？

⑰ Any suggestions you have would be much appreciated. 　您有任何建议，我都十分感激。

⑱ I'd appreciate hearing any suggestions you have. 　很感谢您给我们提的建议。

⑲ Your advice is always very valuable to me. 　您的建议对我总是很有价值。

⑳ I would be very grateful for your advice. 　我很感谢您的建议。

给出建议 *Offering suggestions*

❶ You should take a vacation and relax. 　你应该休假好好放松一下。

❷ Talking to your boss would probably be a good idea. 　跟你的老板谈谈可能是个好主意。

❸ I think you should do whatever you're most comfortable with. 　我想你应该做最适合你的事情。

❹ If you're worried about safety in your neighborhood, why not install a home security system? 　如果你担心附近安全的话，为什么不装一个家庭安全系统？

❺ If the two of you are arguing all the time, maybe you're not meant to be together. 　如果你们俩总吵架，你们可能就不该在一起。

❻ Since you've never been to Europe before, I'd recommend going to Italy or France first. 　既然你从未到过欧洲，我建议你先去意大利和法国。

❼ It might be a good idea to start looking for a new job before you resign. 　在你辞职之前就开始找新工作，这是个好主意。

❽ My advice is to look for a new investment advisor. 　我的建议是找一位新的投资顾问。

❾ In this kind of situation, it's best to forgive and forget. 　这种情况下，我们最好能原谅或者遗忘。

❿ If I were you, I would just tell her your true feelings. 　如果我是你，我就告诉她你的真实感受。

⓫ If you want to get more exercise, why not join a gym? 　如果你想多做一些锻炼，为什么不去健身房呢？

⑫ I think you should consider seeing a doctor.   我想你应该考虑去看医生。

⑬ You might want to consult a lawyer.   你可能得咨询律师。

信例 1（生活类）

Hi Max,

I want to ask for your advice on something. My wife and I are thinking about going away on vacation in December to either Cuba or the Bahamas. Since you've been to both countries, I was wondering if you could give us your thoughts. Which do you think would be a better choice for us?

Regards,

Kyle

我有事情想征求你的建议。我和我爱人打算 12 月份去度假，或者去古巴或者去巴哈马。这两个国家你都去过，我想问问你的看法。你觉得我们选择哪个国家更好呢？

信例 2（商务类）

Dear Joel,

I was surprised to hear that you've been having so many disputes with your landlord recently. If he's making unreasonable demands, you may wish to contact your lawyer. Apart from that, I'd also suggest looking for a new apartment well in advance of the lease expiring. It's always best to be prepared for contingencies.

Best wishes,

Claire

听说你和你的房东最近发生了许多争执我很惊讶。如果他的要求不合理，你可以和你的律师联系。除此之外，我还建议你在合同到期前找好新公寓。最好是做充分准备，以防意外。

15 警告 Giving warnings

❶ You should be more careful next time.   下次小心点儿。

❷ Please be more careful in the future.   以后小心点儿。

❸ There's going to be a heavy snowfall today, so be careful driving home tonight.   今天雪下得很大，晚上开车回家路上一定要小心。

❹ If you consume alcohol at the party, just leave your car there and take a taxi home.

如果晚会上喝了酒，你就把车放那，打车回家吧。

❺ If you do not pay this balance within seven days, we will be forced to suspend your service.

如果你 7 天之内不把余额还清，我们就得暂停你的服务。

❻ If we continue to receive complaints about your loud music, we may be forced to evict you.

如果我们还是不断地听到大家抱怨你的音乐声音太大，我们可能要被迫收回房屋。

❼ If you are absent for the next meeting without a valid reason, you may become ineligible for your annual bonus.

如果下次会议你还是没有合理的理由就缺席的话，你可能就没有年终奖了。

❽ If you keep calling my house, I will report you to the authorities.

如果你不断地往我家打电话，我就会到相关部门去告你。

❾ Make sure you bring lots of warm clothes for the winter in Moscow.

冬天到莫斯科一定要带许多厚衣服。

❿ Bring lots of sunscreen when you go to Hainan Island.

你去海南岛的时候要多带防晒油。

⓫ You could have gotten into a lot of trouble.

你们很可能碰上一堆麻烦。

⓬ I hope I won't have to warn you again.

我希望不用警告你第二次。

信例 1（生活类）

Hi Jane,

I heard you're planning a trip to Harbin during the Spring Festival. Just make sure you pack your warmest clothing … the winter temperatures there can drop down to –20 degrees. I was underdressed when I went last year and came back with a nasty cold. Stay warm and you'll have a fantastic time.

Best regards,

Nick

我听说你正准备春节期间去哈尔滨旅行。一定要带上你最保暖的衣服。冬天那里的气温能降到零下 20 度。我去年去那儿衣服穿少了，回来感冒很严重。穿得暖和点儿，你会玩儿得格外开心。

Dear Mr. Smith,

Yesterday was the second time this month that you were absent from a planning meeting. We understand that you have a long commute in the morning. However, you should be aware that these meetings are mandatory. If you are absent from the next meeting, we will be forced to take disciplinary action.

Sincerely,

Nancy Jones

昨天已经是您这个月第二次缺席策划会议了。您早晨路途很远，我们很理解。但是您应该知道这些会议是必须到场的。如果您下次会议仍然缺席的话，我们将只能给您纪律处分了。

16 劝说 Giving advice

❶ I'm not sure that's the best decision. 　　我不认为这是最好的决定。

❷ I think you should reconsider. 　　我想你应该再考虑考虑。

❸ How can I persuade you to change your mind? 　　我怎么才能劝你改变想法呢？

❹ There's still time to change your mind. 　　你要改变主意还来得及。

❺ Just consider all your options before making a decision. 　　在做出决定前要把你所有的选择都考虑进去。

❻ You're going to burn out if you keep working so hard. 　　如果你一直这么辛苦工作的话，你的身体会垮掉的。

❼ Personally, I would advise against it. 　　就我而言，我会建议不这样做。

❽ I would advise you to quit smoking. 　　我劝你戒烟。

Dear Eugene,

It concerns me to see you missing so many classes and falling behind in your coursework. Whatever difficulties you're experiencing, it's not worth abandoning your college studies. I'd be glad to meet with you to discuss how we can help you get back on the track. It's not too late to turn your marks around.

Sincerely,

Linda Clark

看到你缺了很多课，成绩也落在了后面，我很担心。无论你面临什么困难，都不值得放弃学业。我很想见见你，跟你谈谈我们怎么能帮你回到正路。扭转你的分数现在还来得及。

信例2（商务类）

Dear Alex,

Before approving the website design, I would advise you to consider adding a Chinese version. Many of our clients are in China, and it wouldn't hurt to have our website accessible in their native language. I know this would add to the overall cost, but the long-term benefit would probably outweigh the short-term expense.

Best regards,

Olivia

在您批准这个网站设计之前，我想建议您考虑增加中文版。我们的许多客户在中国，用他们的母语进入我们的网站是没有什么坏处的。我知道这可能会增加总成本，但是它的长期收益一定会超过这短期的花费。

第三部分　表明态度
Expressing Attitudes

17 表达愿望 Expressing wishes

❶ I really wish I could see him/her again. 　　我真希望能再次见到他/她。

❷ I hope I can see you again. 　　我希望我能再次见到你。

❸ I wish I could be young again. 　　真希望我能再年轻一次。

❹ My greatest wish is to become a doctor/ lawyer/journalist/singer. 　　我最大的愿望就是成为一名医生/律师/记者/歌手。

❺ I aspire to be a great teacher/artist/ writer/photographer. 　　我渴望成为一名出色的教师/艺术家/作者/摄影师。

❻ I really hope I get accepted to law/ medical school. 　　我真希望我能考入法学院/医学院。

❼ I'll be ecstatic if I get this job! 　　我要是能得到这份工作，会高兴死的。

❽ I hope you're feeling better soon. 　　我希望你很快好转起来。

信例1（生活类）

Hi Maria,

Can you believe graduation is just around the corner? The past four years have gone by in a flash. I've applied for several jobs, but the one I'm really hoping for is the systems analyst position at Triple-Biotech Corp. I'm keeping my fingers crossed! Have you figured out your plans for next year yet?

With best regards,

Vincent

你能相信马上就要毕业了吗？过去的四年弹指一挥间，我已经申请了几份工作，但我真正期待的是三博生物科技有限公司的系统分析员的职位。我一直在祈祷。你为明年做了哪些计划呢？

信例 2（商务类）

Dear Keith,

Marie told me that you called in sick this morning with a bad cold. I know you're worried about this week's deadline, but we can assign someone else to finish the report. Please take as much time off as you need and get plenty of rest. I hope you're feeling better soon.

Sincerely,

Miranda

玛丽告诉我说你感冒很严重，今天早晨打电话请了病假。我知道你很担心这周的最后期限，我们可以安排别人完成这个报告。你需要多长时间就请多长时间假，好好休息。希望你很快好起来。

18 说明意向 Stating intentions

❶ I'm planning to buy a house in the suburbs. 　　我想在郊区买套房子。

❷ I'm thinking about buying a new television. 　　我一直想买个新电视。

❸ I've decided to spend my winter vacation in Florida. 　　我决定去佛罗里达州过寒假。

❹ My cousin and I are going to visit the Great Wall on Saturday. 　　我和我表弟周六去参观长城。

❺ I've made up my mind to apply for law/medical school. 　　我已经下定决心申请法学院/医学院。

❻ I'm determined to complete my first novel by the end of the year. 　　我决定年末完成我的第一部小说。

❼ I intend to look for a job after finishing my master's studies. 　　读完硕士后我想找份工作。

❽ I'm going to leave first thing in the morning to avoid rush hour. 　　我找算早晨早点儿出发避开高峰期。

❾ I plan to go backpacking across Europe this summer. 　　我打算今年夏天背包旅行穿越欧洲。

❿ He finally decided to change his college major. 　　他最终决定要改专业。

⓫ She's intent on getting married before her 30th birthday. 　　她坚持要在 30 岁之前结婚。

⓬ I feel like going to the beach this weekend. 　　我这个周末想去海滩。

Hi Pat,

How was your weekend? Most of mine was spent trying to repair my computer—but to no avail. I'm using my girlfriend's laptop to write you this e-mail right now. At any rate, I've decided to go and pick up a new computer sometime soon. If you're not too busy, maybe we could go together?

Regards,

David

周末过得怎么样？我大部分时间都用来修电脑了，但还是没修好。我现在用的是我女朋友的笔记本给你写的邮件，不管怎么说我决定最近要买一台新电脑。如果你不是很忙的话，我们一起去怎么样？

Dear Ben,

I just wanted to let you know that I've decided to move back to California next month. I've been in Chicago for almost a year and I really like it here, but most of my family is in L. A. Anyway, I'll see you this weekend at the convention and we can talk more then.

Regards,

Elizabeth

我就想告诉你我已经决定下个月搬回加利福尼亚州了。我在芝加哥待了一年了，我真的很喜欢这里，可是我的家人大部分都在洛杉矶。不管怎么说，这个周末的大会上我能见到你，到时候我们再详谈。

19 表达重要性 Expressing importance

❶ You're very important to me. 你对我非常重要。

❷ Your opinion is important to me. 你的观点对我来说很重要。

❸ This is an extremely crucial/important matter. 这是极其关键的/重要的问题。

❹ First impressions are very/extremely important. 第一印象非常/极其重要。

⑤ It's vital that you attend tomorrow's meeting.

明天的会议你要出席这很关键。

⑥ Actions speak louder than words.

行动胜于言辞。

⑦ The success of this project is imperative to the company's future.

这个项目成功与否对公司的前景至关重要。

⑧ The author argues that good health is more important than money.

作者认为身体好比金钱重要得多。

⑨ A positive attitude is the key to success.

积极的态度是成功的关键。

⑩ Losing such a small contract is of little consequence to us.

失去这么个小订单对我们没什么大不了的。

⑪ What happened in the past is unimportant.

过去发生什么不重要。

⑫ You needn't pay attention to such inconsequential details.

你无需对那些无关痛痒的细节特别注意。

⑬ What other people think isn't that important to me.

别人怎么想对我不重要。

⑭ I suppose it doesn't really matter.

我觉得这个无关紧要。

⑮ It's of no significance to me.

这个对我没有任何意义。

信例 1（生活类）

Hey Joseph,

I was pretty disappointed last week about not getting into law school. But after our conversation, I realized that it's not really a big deal. I have a few good job offers, and I'm not particularly keen on going back to school for another three years anyway. Thanks for helping me see the light.

With gratitude,

Sandy

没能进入法学院我上周非常失望。但是和你谈完之后，我意识到这也没什么大不了的。我有几个很好的工作机会，再说我也不是特别想回学校再读三年。非常感谢，你的话让我豁然开朗。

信例 2（商务类）

Dear Patricia,

I looked over your draft of the feasibility study and you've done a thorough job. I just have two small suggestions. First, let's expand on the recommendations to make them more prominent. Second, the introduction is good but I think it could be more concise. Please send me another copy once you've made these changes.

Thanks,

Greg

你的可行性研究草案我从头到尾通读了一遍，你分析得很彻底。我只有两点小的建议：第一，对于可取之处我们再拓展一些，使它们更加突出。第二，导言部分写得很好，但它可以再简洁些。你做完修改再发给我一份。

20 表示有能力 Expressing ability

❶ I can get the job done by myself. | 我自己能把工作干完。
❷ We can definitely finish the project by tomorrow. | 我明天肯定能完成这个项目。
❸ I have the ability to stay focused for long periods of time. | 我能够长时间地集中精力。
❹ He's fluent in Spanish and Italian. | 他西班牙语和意大利语说得都很流利。
❺ She's a qualified and experienced piano teacher. | 她是个资历很深而且很有教学经验的钢琴老师。
❻ I can type about 100 words per minute. | 我每分钟能打大约 100 个字。
❼ I can probably fix your computer. | 我很可能修好你的电脑。

信例 1（生活类）

Hi Dorothy,

I just got your message about your car not starting. Have you called a mechanic yet? I'll be off work tomorrow morning, so I could drop by your place and have a look at it. If it's a minor problem, I might be able to fix it for you. Call me and let me know.

Kind regards,

Charles

我刚收到你的消息说你的车启动不了了。你打电话叫修理工了吗？明早我不上班，我可以在你那停一下看看怎么回事，如果是小毛病，我自己就能给你修好。给我回电话。

信例2（商务类）

Dear Mr. Davis,
I understand that you have been looking for someone to compile and edit our office's monthly newsletter. If the position hasn't yet been filled, I would like to offer to serve as editor. I'm aware of the time commitment involved, but I'm confident that I can handle it and do a good job.
Sincerely,
Gerard Hall

我知道您一直在找人撰写和编辑我们办公室的每月时事通讯。如果该职位仍然空缺，我很愿意做编辑为您效劳。我知道这份工作需要保证时间，但是我有信心处理好它，能够很好地完成工作。

21 请求许可 Asking permission

请求许可 Asking for permission

❶ Could I borrow your library card tomorrow? 　你明天能把图书卡借我吗？

❷ Would it be alright if I copied your lecture notes? 　我可以复印你的课堂笔记吗？

❸ Would you mind if I borrowed your car for the weekend? 　您介意我这周末借用您的车吗？

❹ Can we bring additional guests to the graduation ceremony? 　我们可以带其他的客人参加毕业典礼吗？

❺ Do you have any objection to my posting your essay on the Internet? 　您反对我把您的论文放在网上吗？

❻ I would like to request permission to reprint an excerpt from your article. 　我希望您能允许再版您文章的节选。

❼ I hope you'll allow me to accompany you on your trip. 　我希望能陪您旅行。

❽ Do I have your permission to speak with him about this issue? 　您能允许我跟他谈谈这个问题吗？

❾ I was wondering if my husband/wife could also attend. 　我想知道我的丈夫/妻子是否也可以参加。

❿ Please let me know if I have your permission. 　如果您允许的话请告知我。

⓫ I would really/greatly appreciate it. 　我真的十分感激。

表示允许 *Granting permission*

① I have no objections to that. 　　　　我不反对。

② You may bring up to three guests to the event. 　　你可以带三位客人参加这次活动。

③ You can definitely borrow my car for the weekend. 　　你周末当然可以借我的车。

④ You have my permission to publish the photographs on your website. 　　你可以在你的网站上发布我的照片。

⑤ I'll give you a one-week extension on the essay deadline. 　　我给你的论文期限延长一周。

⑥ Feel free to reprint my article for classroom use. 　　你可以重印我的文章供上课使用。

⑦ You can borrow my driver's license, but I'll need it back by Friday. 　　我可以借给你我的驾照，但你周五前必须还我。

⑧ You're welcome to use my laptop tomorrow. 　　你明天可以使用我的手提电脑。

⑨ That would be perfectly fine with me. 　　那对我太方便了。

⑩ You have my permission. 　　我同意。

表示不允许 *Denying permission*

① I'm sorry, but I can't change the rules. 　　对不起，我不能改变规定。

② I'm afraid that the meeting is mandatory for all employees. 　　恐怕所有的员工必须出席会议。

③ The final project is mandatory for all students. 　　所有的学生都必须上交最终的方案。

④ Unfortunately, you cannot be exempted from the examination. 　　很抱歉，你不能免考。

⑤ I'm afraid I can't lend you my car until you have a driver's license. 　　恐怕得等你有了驾照，我才能借你车。

⑥ For security reasons, we cannot give you access to that information. 　　鉴于安全问题，我们还不能让你知道那些信息。

⑦ Access to this website is restricted to members only. 　　只有会员才能进入这个网站。

⑧ We can't disclose any information about this case until it is settled. 　　在事情未解决之前，我们不能透漏任何信息。

⑨ Since there is still so much unfinished work, I'm afraid I can't give you the day off.

因为这有很多没完成的工作，所以恐怕我不能给你假。

⑩ Because of the limited number of seats, you are not allowed to bring any guests.

由于座位数量有限，你们不能带客人来。

⑪ It would be unfair to the other students to give you an extension.

给你延期对其他同学来说是不公平的。

⑫ There is a regulation prohibiting pets in this building.

有规定楼内不许养宠物。

⑬ I don't have the authority to grant your request.

我没有权力同意你的要求。

⑭ I'm afraid there are no exceptions.

恐怕不能有例外。

信例1（生活类）

Hi Mark,

It was great to see you and Alice on Saturday. Jen and I are celebrating our two-year anniversary next weekend, and we're planning a trip to Sacramento. If you don't mind, could we borrow your convertible from Friday to Sunday? If it's not convenient, we can always rent a car. I just thought I'd ask.

Cheers,

James

很高兴周六见到了你和爱丽丝。詹和我下周想去萨克拉门托旅行，庆祝我们结婚两周年。如果你们不介意的话，周五到周日能借给我们你的折篷汽车吗？如果不方便的话，我们就租辆车。我只是想问一下。

信例2（商务类）

Dear Ms. Stewart,

With regard to your e-mail of May 8, I'm glad to grant you permission to use an excerpt from my article in your seminar and any related handouts. Your offer of compensation, although appreciated, is really unnecessary. Allow me to wish you the best of luck on your seminar.

Yours sincerely,

Dr. Clement Zhang

关于你5月8日的邮件，我很高兴地告诉你，你可以在你们的研讨会上引用我文章的内容和使用任何相关印刷品。你提到给与报酬，我很感激，但真的不用。祝你们的研讨会好运、成功。

22 应该不应该 Should I or shouldn't I?

❶ I should have registered for my courses earlier. 我应该早点儿注册我的课程。

❷ I shouldn't have stayed up so late last night. 我昨晚不该熬夜到那么晚。

❸ I really shouldn't have divulged my friend's secret. 我真不应该把我朋友的秘密泄露出去。

❹ I feel that it's my responsibility to help him. 我觉得帮助他是我的责任。

❺ I think you ought to tell her the truth. 我看你应该告诉她事实。

❻ Should I send you the report when I finish writing it? 我写完之后应该把报告给你发过去吗?

❼ Since I broke your camera, it's only fair that I buy you a new one. 我弄坏了你的照相机，应该给你买台新的才公平。

❽ I think I should ask my professor for an extension on the essay. 我想我应该问问我老师论文延期的事。

❾ I don't think you should take the first job offer you get. 我认为你不该要你得到的第一份工作。

❿ I don't know if we'll succeed or fail, but we should at least do our best. 我不知道我们胜败如何，但至少我们做了最大的努力。

⓫ I can't decide whether I should continue with my studies or look for a job. 我还没有决定我是应该继续我的学业还是找工作。

⓬ I'm not sure whether I should switch to a different service provider or not. 我不知道我是否应该另换一个服务商。

⓭ Are there any vaccinations I should get before visiting Southeast Asia? 在访问东南亚之前，我需要接种一些疫苗吗?

⓮ Am I supposed to finish preparing the slideshow today? 我今天应该准备好幻灯片吗?

⓯ Do you think I should buy a house? 您认为我该买套房子吗?

⓰ I'm wondering if I should consult a lawyer. 我在考虑我是否应该请律师。

Hi Brad,

You're studying abroad next semester too, right? Do you know whether we need to have the courses we intend to take approved by our faculty in advance? I got an e-mail from the registrar's office that may have addressed this question, but I deleted it by mistake! Please call me when you have a chance.

Thanks,

Yolanda

你下学期也要去国外学习是吗？你知道我们想要学的课程是否需要事先得到学院的批准吗？我收到一封来自注册老师办公室的邮件，可能是针对这一问题的，但是我不小心把它删了，你要是知道请告诉我。

Dear Julian,

Although tomorrow's conference is not mandatory, you are still strongly encouraged to attend. It's a valuable chance to gain some insight into developments and trends in the food and beverage industry. If you have plans in the afternoon, you could still consider attending the morning session from 8:30 to 11:00 am.

Sincerely,

Kate Olson

虽然明天的会议不是必须到场，但我们还是非常希望您能参加。这是一次极为宝贵的机会，您可以深入了解一些餐饮业的发展趋势。如果您下午有事的话，仍然可以考虑参加上午的分会，8 点半开始 11 点结束。

23 赞同和不赞同 Agreeing and disagreeing

表示强烈赞同 *Expressing strong agreement*

❶ I totally/completely agree with you.　我完全同意你的观点。

❷ I agree with you 100 percent.　我完全同意你。

❸ I couldn't agree more.　我完全赞同。

❹ I fully agree that we should expand into the Asian market.　我完全同意我们应该扩展亚洲市场。

❺ We see completely eye to eye on these issues.　我们对这些问题的意见完全一致。

❻ I'm in full agreement with you on that point. 这一点我完全同意你的看法。

❼ I'm of the exact same opinion as you. 我的看法和你一模一样。

❽ What you said is absolutely right. 你说得完全正确。

表示赞同 Expressing agreement

❶ I agree with you. 我同意你。

❷ I'm in agreement with you. 我同意你。

❸ I'm of the same opinion as you. 我和你看法一致。

❹ I support your position on this issue. 在这个问题上我和你观点相同。

❺ I support your views on this matter. 在这个问题上我支持你的观点。

❻ I think what you say is makes sense. 我觉得你说得有道理。

❼ I concur with your point of view. 我同意你的观点。

❽ I don't have any objections. 我没有任何意见。

❾ I agree with you on that point. 在这一点上我赞同你。

❿ You made a good point there. 你的想法很好。

⓫ I think that's a good idea. 我觉得这是个好主意。

有保留地赞同 Agreeing with reservations

❶ I basically agree with you. 我基本上同意你。

❷ My opinion is almost the same as yours. 我想法和你的差不多。

❸ I agree with most of what you said. 你说的大部分我都赞同。

❹ I agree with you for the most part. 大部分我都同意。

❺ I guess you're right. 我想你说得对。

不同意 Expressing disagreement

❶ I disagree with you. 我不同意你的看法。

❷ I totally/completely disagree with you. 我完全不同意。

❸ I don't/can't agree with your comments. 我不赞同你的观点。

❹ I'm afraid I don't quite agree. 恐怕我不能同意你。

❺ I'm going to have to disagree with you. 我将不会同意你。

❻ My viewpoint is somewhat different from yours. 我的观点和你的不同。

❼ You couldn't be further from the truth. 你离事实越来越远了。

❽ Our views differ on this issue. 在这个问题上我们的观点不同。

❾ I don't agree with what you said about the author's writing style. 我不同意你说的关于作者写作风格的看法。

⑩ I know you didn't like that movie, but I really enjoyed it. 　　我知道你不喜欢那个电影，但我真是迷上它了。

⑪ That's not how I see it. 　　我并不这么认为。

信例1（生活类）

Hey Lily,

I agree with you that we should meet for at least one more practice session before the competition. I think we're relatively well-prepared at this point, but I'm sure the other teams are in pretty good shape, too. I'll call the rest of the guys and see if they have time this weekend.

Kind regards,

Andrew

我很赞同你说的我们应该在比赛前至少再练一次。我觉得目前我们准备得比较好，但我相信对手准备得也很充分。我会给其他人打电话看看他们这周末是否有时间。

信例2（商务类）

Hi Scott,

The boss is expecting us to finish the market analysis tomorrow, so I don't think we should go to the bar tonight. The last time we went out for drinks on a weeknight you got really tanked and came in late the next day. How about we go out Friday evening instead?

Regards,

Patrick

老板希望我们明天完成市场分析，所以我觉得我们今晚不应该去酒吧。上次我们工作日晚上去喝酒，你喝醉了而且第二天上班迟到了。我们周五晚上再去吧，怎么样？

---

24 喜欢和不喜欢 Likes and dislikes

喜欢 Likes

❶ I like going for a jog first thing in the morning. 　　我喜欢早晨一起来就出去慢跑。

❷ I like reading Shakespearean sonnets. 　　我喜欢看莎士比亚的十四行诗。

③ Basketball is one of my favorite sports. 篮球是我最喜欢的体育项目。

④ I enjoy going camping in the wilderness. 我喜欢在荒野中宿营。

⑤ I have a particular fondness for Italian red wine. 我特别喜欢意大利红酒。

⑥ He's also a keen chess player. 他也是一位精明的棋手。

⑦ She's a real chocoholic! 她真是一个巧克力迷!

⑧ I'm fond of both cats and dogs. 猫狗我都喜欢。

⑨ There's nothing I like more than a good debate. 没有什么比精彩的辩论更让我喜欢的了。

⑩ I'm an avid fan of science fiction novels. 我是个科幻小说迷。

⑪ We both like playing soccer and table tennis. 我们都喜欢踢足球和打乒乓球。

不喜欢 Dislikes

① I don't care much for violent movies. 我不喜欢暴力影片。

② I dislike spicy and greasy foods. 我不喜欢吃辛辣的、油腻的食品。

③ I've never liked playing sports. 我从不喜欢运动。

④ He has an aversion to snakes and spiders. 我讨厌蛇和蜘蛛。

⑤ She hates it when other people interrupt her. 她很讨厌别人打断她。

⑥ I'm not too keen on country music. 我不是特别喜欢乡村音乐。

⑦ I'm not a big fan of computer games. 我不是很喜欢玩儿电脑游戏。

信例1（生活类）

Hi Peter,
I heard you're taking a trip to Switzerland over the spring break. I love everything about that country: the Swiss Alps, Swiss chocolate, Swiss cheese ... I really wish I could go with you. But I'll be going there this summer anyway, so I suppose there's no hurry. Hope you have a great time!
Ciao,
Sheryl

我听说开春你要去瑞士旅行。对那个国家我真是什么都喜欢：瑞士的阿尔卑斯山、瑞士巧克力、瑞士奶酪……我真希望能和你一起去。不过这个夏天我会去那的，所以我想也不用着急。祝你玩儿得开心！

Dear Adam,

Yesterday we got one of those deluxe coffee machines installed at the office. Everyone was racing to it first thing this morning as if their lives depended on it. Personally, I'm not big on coffee, but I know what a coffee aficionado you are. Now you'll have something to look forward to when you come back.

Regards,

Isabelle

昨天我们买了一款豪华咖啡机安装在办公室里。大家今早一来都迫不及待地去使用它，好像他们的生命就靠它了一样。我不大喜欢咖啡，但我知道你可是咖啡狂热者。这下你回来就能用上你想要的东西了。

25 表示偏爱 Expressing preferences

❶ I find taking the train much more convenient than traveling by air.　我觉得坐火车比乘飞机旅行方便多了。

❷ I prefer Chinese food to Korean food.　我更喜欢中餐，不喜欢韩国餐。

❸ When I go downtown, I like to take a taxi rather than go by subway.　我愿意打车去市区，不愿意乘地铁。

❹ I like to walk to school as opposed to taking the bus, except during bad weather.　除了天气不好的时候，平时我都喜欢走着去学校，而不愿意坐公交车。

❺ Jogging is my preferred form of exercise.　慢跑是我比较喜欢的锻炼方式。

❻ As far as I'm concerned, it's more convenient to live in the city than in the countryside.　就我而言，住在城市比住在乡村方便得多。

❼ In my opinion, nothing is more relaxing than going for a walk on the beach.　在我看来，没有比海滩漫步更让人轻松的事情了。

❽ I think shopping online is easier than going to the mall.　我觉得网上购物比去商场购物要方便得多。

❾ I usually like to travel to Switzerland or Austria on my vacation.　我假期很想去瑞士或者奥地利旅行。

信例 1（生活类）

Hey Isaac,

Have you thought about where we can go for dinner tomorrow? I have Western food all the time, so I usually prefer something exotic when eating out. Have you been to any of the Thai or Vietnamese restaurants downtown? Let me know your thoughts. Looking forward to seeing you soon!

Yours truly,

Sarah

你想好我们明天去哪吃晚餐了吗？我天天都吃西餐，所以这次我想出去吃点儿有异国情调的。你去过市中心的泰国或者越南餐馆吗？告诉我你的想法。

希望很快就能见到你。

信例 2（商务类）

Dear Mario,

I've booked our hotel accommodations for the IT exhibition in Florida. We just need to arrange the transportation now. Would you rather travel by plane or bus? The price difference between the two is almost negligible. I would be fine either way, so let me know your preference and I'll make the arrangements.

Regards,

Jerome

我已经为去佛罗里达州 IT 展览会预订了宾馆住宿。现在只需安排交通工具了。你愿意坐飞机还是坐大巴呢？价钱差不多，我什么都行，看你更喜欢哪种方式，然后告诉我，我好安排。

26 表示兴趣 Expressing interest

询问他人是否对某事物感兴趣 *Asking about the other's interests*

1 Are you interested in sci-fi novels? 你对科幻小说感兴趣吗？

2 Are you interested in foreign movies? 你对国外影片感兴趣吗？

3 What are your interests? 你对什么感兴趣？

4 What interests do you have? 你有什么兴趣爱好？

5 Would you be interested in going to a concert with me? 你愿意跟我一起去听音乐会吗？

⑥ Would you be up for a trip to Thailand this summer? 你今年夏天想去泰国旅行吗?

⑦ Does Latin music interest you at all? 你对拉丁音乐感兴趣吗?

⑧ I was wondering if you might be interested in volunteering. 我想知道你是否对志愿者活动感兴趣?

⑨ Does Beijing opera appeal to you? 你喜欢京剧吗?

表达对某事物感兴趣 *Expressing an interest*

① I'm interested in Spanish and Portuguese. 我对西班牙语和葡萄牙语感兴趣。

② I have a strong interest in philosophy. 我对哲学有浓厚的兴趣。

③ I'm definitely interested in going to the concert with you. 我非常想和你一起去听音乐会。

④ I'm interested in attending the seminar this weekend. 我很想参加这周末的学术研讨会。

⑤ I'm particularly/especially interested in Freudian psychology. 我对弗洛伊德心理学特别感兴趣。

⑥ I've been interested in science since I was young. 我从小对科学感兴趣。

⑦ He is fascinated by ancient Greek architecture. 他对古希腊式建筑非常感兴趣。

⑧ She is very interested in Chinese history. 她对中国历史很感兴趣。

表达对某事物不感兴趣 *Expressing a lack of interest*

① I'm not interested in watching TV sitcoms. 我不想看电视情景喜剧。

② To tell you the truth, I'm not very interested in classical music. 说实话,我对古典音乐不太感兴趣。

③ I'm not at all interested in geography. 我对地理学一点儿兴趣也没有。

④ I have no interest in modern art. 我对现代艺术没有兴趣。

⑤ I'm not really interested in seeing that movie. 我不是很想看那部电影。

⑥ I've never been interested in zoology. 我对动物学从来不感兴趣。

Hi Cindy,

There's a cooking class being offered on weekends this summer ... I'm thinking about signing up for it. I'm a total novice in the kitchen, but I've always wanted to learn the culinary arts. Are you interested at all in cooking? If you are, maybe we could go and sign up together.

Warmest regards,

Vivian

今年夏天每个周末都有烹饪课，我一直想报名。我下厨什么都不会，但是我总想学学烹饪艺术。你对烹饪感兴趣吗？如果你也喜欢，我们可以一起去报名。

Dear Tara,

I just got your voice mail. Which movies were you planning to see at the film festival? I'm not really an avid filmgoer, but I do like foreign films. I browsed the festival schedule online and I think that Italian comedy might be interesting. What do you think? Have you read any reviews for it?

Best regards,

Daniel

我刚刚收到你的语音邮件。电影节你都打算看哪些电影呢？我不是电影迷，但我确实喜欢外国影片。我在网上浏览了电影节安排，我觉得意大利喜剧可能会很有意思。你觉得呢？你读过它的影评吗？

27 表示不确定 Expressing uncertainty

❶ I doubt the veracity of his statement.   我觉得他的话不可信。

❷ I'm doubtful that she can finish the project on time.   我怀疑她是否能按时完成这个项目。

❸ I'm having doubts about our ability to get the job done.   我怀疑我们是否有能力完成这项工作。

❹ I suspect that we may have made a mistake.   我觉得我们可能犯了个错误。

⑤ I have my suspicions about whether the stock price will rise.

我怀疑股票价格是否会上涨。

⑥ I'm not sure whether this product design is feasible.

我不确定这个产品设计是否可行。

⑦ Because of his lack of confidence, he always feels uncertain about his decisions.

因为他缺乏信心，所以他对自己的决定总是心里没数。

⑧ She's having second thoughts about her relationship with Quentin.

她在重新考虑她和昆廷的关系。

⑨ It's not certain whether they can win the tournament.

他们能不能赢得这次锦标赛还不确定。

⑩ I don't know whether management can turn around the company's losses.

我不知道管理者是否能扭转公司的损失。

⑪ I'm not too optimistic about our chances of getting the contract.

对于我们能否拿到合同我还不是很乐观。

⑫ My lawyer expects me to receive a large settlement, but I have my doubts.

我的律师预计我能收到一大笔财产，但我不大相信。

⑬ I have the feeling that Rachel's marks aren't as high as she says.

我觉得蕾切尔的分数不像她说得那么高。

⑭ I question whether Sam will follow through on his commitment.

我怀疑塞姆是否能实现他的承诺。

⑮ There is no certainty about the outcome of the election.

选举的结果还没确定。

⑯ I'm kind of skeptical about the author's theory.

我有点儿怀疑作者的理论。

⑰ I have a hard time believing everything he says.

他说什么我都不大相信。

⑱ Do you really think that her words are credible?

你真觉得她的话可信吗？

⑲ I'll do my best, but I doubt that I can solve your problem.

我会尽最大的努力，但我看未必能解决你的问题。

⑳ I'm not sure whether I can help you.

我不知道我能不能帮上你。

信例 1（生活类）

Hi Larry,

I've met with several potential sponsors during the last two weeks, but the results so far have been disappointing. I'm just not sure whether we'll be able to meet our club's fundraising target. I know you don't want to increase membership fees, but we need to find a way to stay above water.

Regards,

Julie

上两周我会见了几个潜在的赞助商，但到目前为止结果太令人失望了。我不确定我们能否达到俱乐部的筹款目标，我知道你不想提高会费，但是我们需要找到一种方法使我们不陷入困境。

信例 2（商务类）

Dear Randy,

I had a chance to look over the new product design that you drafted. Although the redesign possesses technical and aesthetic enhancements, you should consider the substantial increase in manufacturing costs that it would entail. I doubt that management will approve the new design unless costs can be kept reasonably low.

Sincerely,

Edward Li

我看了你草拟的新产品设计，尽管在技术上和艺术上都有改观，但你需要考虑它在生产成本上的实质增加。我觉得如果成本不能降得比较低的话，领导们不会同意这个新的设计方案。

28 责怪和抱怨 Blaming and complaining

❶ How many times do I have to tell you?　我得跟你说多少次？

❷ I'm getting tired of always having to remind you.　我总得提醒你，我都厌烦了。

❸ This is the third time you've made the same mistake.　这已经是你第三次犯同样的错误了。

❹ I've had enough of your constant complaining.　我听够了你没完没了的抱怨。

❺ You really need to improve your negative attitude.　你真该改改你的消极态度。

⑥ I don't think I can tolerate this behavior any more.
我觉得我再也不能忍受你的行为了。

⑦ I've asked you several times to finish the report already.
我已经跟你说了几次把报告写完。

⑧ I would like to make a complaint about your customer service.
我想投诉你们的客服。

⑨ I waited over three hours for the technician, but he didn't show up.
我等那个技术工人等了 3 个多小时，可他还没出现呢。

⑩ I can't believe she would go back on her word like that.
她都这么说了，我觉得她不会回来了。

⑪ The website has been down for over an hour now.
这个网页出了故障，都一个多小时了。

⑫ I think you overcharged me for the translation work.
我觉得这个翻译工作你向我要价高了。

⑬ When you make a promise, you should keep it.
你既然答应了，你就要遵守诺言。

⑭ I've almost reached my boiling point.
我快气疯了。

信例 1（生活类）

Dear Barry,
I have to say that I'm disappointed in you. I was glad to lend you my laptop for the weekend, but it's already Tuesday and you still haven't returned it. If you needed to borrow it for another few days, it would have been common courtesy to ask me first. Please return it to me by tomorrow.
Samantha

我得说我对你太失望了。我很乐意这个周末把笔记本电脑借给你，但是现在已经是周二了，你还没还给我。如果你想再借几天，你要先问问我这是最起码的礼貌。明天请把笔记本还给我。

信例 2（商务类）

Dear Sir or Madam,
I wish to make a formal complaint. Last month, I contacted your office requesting that my phone number be removed from your calling list. Despite this, I've received multiple sales calls during the past week. I'm discouraged by your newspaper's lack of professionalism, and I expect this problem to be rectified immediately.
Sincerely,
Harold Bailey

我想投诉。上个月，我与你们办公室联系过，要求把我的手机号从电话表上删除。尽管如此，上周我还是接到了许多推销电话。你们的报纸太缺乏职业精神了，我很失望。我希望你们立即解决这件事情。

第四部分　可能程度
Degree of Possibility

29 肯定和不肯定 Certainty and uncertainty

肯定　*Certainty*

❶ I'm positive I've seen him somewhere before.　　我肯定之前在哪见过你。

❷ I'm fully confident that she'll do a superb job.　　我绝对相信她会做得非常出色。

❸ I'm certain that Tony will get into law/medical school.　　我肯定托尼能进法学院/医学院。

❹ I have no doubt that Vivian will follow through on her promise.　　我相信薇薇安能够遵循她的承诺。

❺ There's absolutely no doubt in my mind.　　我的想法里绝对没有疑问。

❻ I know that you'll have a great time.　　我知道你过得很快乐。

❼ We'll definitely see each other this summer.　　这个夏天我们肯定能见面的。

不肯定　*Uncertainty*

❶ I'm not completely sure about that.　　那件事情我不是很有把握。

❷ I don't know whether the schedule is feasible.　　我不知道这个日程表是否可行。

❸ I wish I were more certain.　　我希望我能更自信些。

❹ I'm not sure whether I've made the right decision.　　我不知道我是否做出了正确的决定。

❺ The plans haven't been confirmed yet.　　这些计划还没有被批准。

❻ It's still unclear whether they can work together as a team.　　我们能不能像一个团队似的在一起工作还不清楚。

❼ There are no guarantees in life.　　在生活中没有保证。

信例1（生活类）

Hi Alison,

As it happens, I know for a fact that Carl doesn't have a girlfriend. If you don't believe me, you can ask any of his friends. I think you should just go ahead and ask him out. If you hesitate for too long, you might find that your chance is gone.

Yours,

Christine

事情就是这样的，我知道卡尔没有女朋友，肯定没错。如果你不相信我，你可以问他任何一个朋友。我想你就应该直接去找他，约他出来。如果你左思右想地犹豫不决，时间一长，你会错过机会的。

信例2（商务类）

Dear Jeffrey,

I'm unconvinced that we'll be able to finish the software by our December 1 deadline. There are only two weeks remaining and we haven't even beta-tested yet. Rather than risking potential glitches in the software, maybe it would be best for us to push back the release date to January. Let me know your opinion.

Regards,

Kenneth

我没有把握我们能在 12 月 1 号的最后期限前完成这个软件。就剩下两周了，我们甚至还没有进行 β 测试。与其冒着软件出现错误的潜在风险，还不如我们最好把发布时间往后延迟到 1 月份。请告之你的想法。

30 可能和不可能 Possibility and impossibility

可能 Possibility

❶ He may start looking for a new job soon. 他可能很快就开始找新工作了。

❷ Her flight might have been delayed. 她的飞机可能晚点了。

❸ There might be a heavy snowfall this weekend. 这周末可能有强烈地降雪。

❹ I think our team has a chance of winning the championship this season. 我想我们队可能有机会赢得这个赛季的冠军。

❺ It's possible that he'll be promoted to CEO within the next year. 他可能明年会被提升为 CEO。

❻ Studying abroad is a possibility I'm considering.　　到国外学习是我正在考虑的一种可能性。

❼ Maybe I'll move to Sweden after I retire.　　退休后我可能搬到瑞典。

不可能 *Impossibility*

❶ There's no way that we can possibly finish before the deadline.　　我们不可能在最后期限前完成。

❷ There's no chance of their team winning the tournament.　　他们队不可能赢得整个联赛。

❸ Unfortunately, I can't be in two places at the same time.　　可惜，我不能在同一时间出现在两个地方。

❹ It's impossible to make a good decision without knowing all the facts.　　不了解所有的事实就做出好决策是不可能的。

❺ I'm sorry, but taking the entire week off is out of the question.　　很抱歉，请整整一星期假绝对不行。

❻ I'm afraid it's not possible for me to go with you on Saturday.　　恐怕周六我不能和你一起去了。

信例1（生活类）

Hi Gloria,

You said your interview tomorrow is at 9 am, right? If you're driving downtown from the suburbs, it'll probably take you at least half an hour to get there. And since there's construction on the freeway, it might take up to an hour during rush hour. I'd leave by 8:00 to be on the safe side.

Good luck,

Justin

你跟我说你明天的面试是在上午9点，对吗？如果你从郊区开车到市中心的话，可能至少半个小时才能到那。但是现在正在修高速路，高峰时间估计得用一个小时。为保险起见，我要8点出发。

Dear Tony,

We received the journal articles that you faxed over and would be glad to translate them into English for you. However, because there are over 100 pages in total, it's unlikely that we could finish by Friday. Would Monday be acceptable? If so, I'll arrange a team of translators to get started right away.

Best regards,

Emily Lin

我们已经收到了您传真过来的报刊文章，我们也很高兴为您翻译成英文。但是总共有一百多页，所以周五全部翻译完不大可能。周一行吗？如果可以的话，我就安排一个翻译小组马上开始翻译。

31 猜测 Guesses

❶ My guess is that this is a technical problem.

我推测这是个技术问题。

❷ Can you speculate as to what the problem might be?

你能想出来问题出在哪儿吗？

❸ It looks like we may be unable to finish by this weekend.

看起来我们到周末也不可能完成。

❹ He appears to have trouble concentrating in class.

他好像上课不能集中精力。

❺ She seems to be firm in her beliefs.

她的信念似乎很坚定。

❻ All we can do is guess.

我们只能猜测罢了。

Hey Craig,

How's your job hunting going? I applied for a clerical position two weeks ago, but still haven't gotten any reply. I'm sure I was well-qualified for the job, so I guess it had already been filled. Fortunately, there's still a month left before graduation.... I'll send in some more applications this week.

Best wishes,

Eileen

你工作找得怎么样？我两周前申请了一个书记员的职位，但到现在还没有回应。我相信我非常胜任这份工作，所以我猜这个职位一定是已经满了。幸好，我们离毕业还有一个月的时间。我这周再投些简历。

信例2（商务类）

Dear Ian,

We sent the samples to the Shenzhen wholesaler almost a week ago, but they haven't confirmed receipt yet. They usually contact us as soon as they receive our products or samples, so it looks like the shipment was delayed. Do you think we should consider switching to a different courier?

Best regards,

William

大约一周前我们给深圳的批发商发了些样品，但是他们到现在还没有确认收到。他们通常都是一收到我们的产品或样品就会和我们联系的，所以这次很可能是运输延迟了。你觉得我们应该考虑换一家货运公司吗？

第五部分　表达情感
Expressing Feelings

32 惊讶 Surprise

❶ What a pleasant/wonderful surprise! 　太令人惊讶了！

❷ This was a total/complete surprise to me. 　对我来说完全是惊喜。

❸ This news comes as a real surprise. 　这个消息确实是个意外。

❹ I never would have expected this to happen. 　我从来都没想到事情会这样。

❺ I was surprised to hear that he didn't get the job. 　听说他没能得到这份工作我很惊讶。

❻ I was shocked at how beautiful she is. 　她太漂亮了，让我惊呆了。

❼ I'm in amazement about this. 　这事让我感到极为惊讶。

❽ His sudden resignation came as a complete shock to us. 　他突然辞职对我们来说如同晴天霹雳。

❾ She surprised herself with her own progress. 　她自己都不敢相信自己取得了这么大的进步。

❿ Everyone was shocked to learn of Will and Yolanda's divorce. 　每个人听说威尔和约兰达离婚都很惊讶。

⓫ My dietician was surprised by my rapid weight loss. 　我能迅速减肥令我的饮食专家都很惊讶。

⓬ I'm still in a state of shock. 　我到现在还很震惊。

⓭ Shall we throw a surprise party for Zack? 　我们给扎克办个出其不意的晚会怎么样？

⓮ I was even more surprised than you. 　我甚至比你更惊讶。

⓯ I'm just as surprised as you are. 　我和你一样惊讶。

⓰ Nothing surprises me anymore. 　已经没有什么事可以让我惊讶了。

Hi Bryce,

I can't believe you're taking flying lessons! I always knew you were the adventurous type ... still, this is a total surprise. When do you start? I really appreciate the invitation to join you, but navigating a plane 2,000 feet above ground isn't my idea of a good time. Have you asked Ruben if he'd be interested?

Regards,

Janet

我真不敢相信您在学习飞行课程，我知道你一直是那种爱冒险的人，可是尽管这样，我还是觉得太意外了。你是什么时候开始上课的？非常感谢你邀请我一起参加，但我不觉得在 2000 英尺的高空开飞机是件令人兴奋的事。你再问问鲁本，看看他是否有兴趣？

Dear John,

I was just as surprised as you at Victor's decision to leave the company. The thing that really stunned me was that he didn't even offer a reason in his resignation letter. After three years of working together, that's the least I would have expected. Anyway, let's meet in the morning to discuss finding a replacement.

Regards,

Amanda

听到维克托决定离开公司，我跟你一样感到惊讶。真正使我震惊的是他在辞职信上甚至都没有写出原因。我们在一起工作 3 年了，这是我最意想不到的事情。不管怎么样，我们明早见个面，讨论一下找个人接替他。

33 好奇 Curiosity

❶ I wonder whether he'll get the promotion.　　我想知道他是否能够提职。

❷ I wonder why she didn't receive the scholarship.　　她没拿到奖学金我很奇怪。

❸ I wonder if the stolen jewelry will ever be recovered.　　我想知道被偷的珠宝还能不能找回来了。

❹ I'm curious about the etymology of many English words.　　我很想把一些英语单词的词形变化弄个明白。

❺ I'm curious about whether he will write any more books.

我很想知道他会不会再写几本书。

❻ I'm curious to know what her reaction will be.

我很想知道她恢复得怎么样了。

❼ I'm curious to know what the outcome of the trial will be.

我很想知道审判的结果是什么。

❽ I'd love to know what the criminal's motive was.

我想弄清楚罪犯的动机是什么。

❾ I'd love to know the identity of the anonymous benefactor.

我很想知道这个匿名的捐赠者是谁。

❿ How in the world was he able to get a perfect score on the test?

他到底是怎么在考试中拿到这么好的成绩呢?

⓫ How on earth did she manage to escape from prison?

她究竟是怎样越狱的呢?

⓬ I can't wait to find out what will happen next.

我等不及要知道接下来会发生什么事。

⓭ I can't wait to find out how the novel ends.

我等不及要知道小说是怎么结尾的。

信例1（生活类）

Hi Kara,

Did you hear about the suicide on campus last night? I wonder who it was and what would compel him to take his own life. There's still police tape up around the student dorm where it happened. I'm just curious to know who the victim is ... I hope it's no one we know.

Take care,

Maggie

你听说昨晚校园里的自杀事件了吗? 我很想知道这个人是谁, 是什么促使他自杀呢? 在事发的学生宿舍, 警察还进行了录音。我只是好奇这个人是谁, 希望不是我认识的人。

Hi Grant,

Did I tell you that I'm being transferred to human resources next week? Since you used to work in that department, I was wondering if you could tell me what to expect from Barbara. Is she tough or easy-going as a manager? I know I'll find out soon enough, but I'm kind of curious.

Regards,

Odette

我告诉过你我下周要调到人力资源部了吗？你过去在这个部门工作，我想问问你芭芭拉这人怎么样？作为经理，她是很严厉的还是很随和的呢？我知道不久我就都知道了，但是我就是有些好奇。

34 高兴 Gladness

❶	That's great/fantastic news.	这是个好消息。
❷	That's wonderful/fantastic/excellent!	那太好了！
❸	This is good news for both of us.	对我们来说都是好消息。
❹	It's always a pleasure to work with you.	跟你一起工作总是很愉快。
❺	I'm delighted to hear that you got the job.	听说你得到了这份工作我很高兴。
❻	I couldn't be happier with the outcome.	我对这个结果感到太高兴了。
❼	I was so glad to see you yesterday.	昨天见到你我很高兴。
❽	I'm really happy for you.	我真为你高兴。

Hi Xiao Yu,

I'm so glad to hear you'll be moving back to Beijing next month! Will it be hard leaving Shanghai after living there for two years? Do you know the exact date you're coming back yet? It'll be great to be able to hang out together again ... I'm really looking forward to seeing you. ：)

Yours,

Chrissie

听说你下个月就搬回北京，我太高兴了。在上海待了两年，离开那里是不是会恋恋不舍？你现在知道回来的具体日期吗？我们又可以一起玩儿了，太好了。我真是迫不及待地见到你。

Dear Ms. Saito,

I want to tell you how pleased we are with the excellent service that your company continues to provide us. We're very grateful for your professional and timely translations, and we've also received positive feedback from many of our Japanese clients. I wish you all the best for a happy holiday season.

Regards,

Agnes Cooper

我想告诉您我们非常满意贵公司提供的优质服务。对于你们专业的、及时的翻译工作我们十分感谢。我们已经收到了许多日本客户的积极反馈。祝你们假期愉快！

35 赞赏 Appreciation and admiration

❶	I admire the richness of Chinese culture.	我钦佩中国文化的博大精深。
❷	I'm really impressed by her creativity.	她的创造力让我印象深刻。
❸	I've long admired him for his wide range of talents.	我一直都很羡慕他广博的才能。
❹	I was impressed by your determination and hard work.	你的坚定和努力给我留下深刻的印象。
❺	Please accept my compliments on your beautiful poem.	你的诗很优美，请接受我的赞赏。
❻	You couldn't have chosen a nicer restaurant for our dinner last night.	昨晚我们吃晚饭的餐馆再好不过了。
❼	Your presentation was educational and inspiring.	你的演讲既有教育意义又令人鼓舞。
❽	You did a terrific/fantastic/superb job.	你干得太棒了。
❾	You've definitely outdone yourself this time.	这次你已经超越了自己。
❿	You've done outstanding/excellent work.	你完成得非常出色。

Hey Justine,

Let me say that your performance in the school play was amazing. I used to think Shakespearean plays were a bit dull, but after watching you last night I'll have to change my opinion. You have a real gift for acting. I wouldn't be surprised to see you on the big screen one day!

Warm regards,

Natalie

我得说你昨天在学校的表演太令人惊叹了，我过去一直认为莎士比亚的戏剧有点儿枯燥，但昨晚看了你的表演，我不得不改变想法。你真是有表演天赋，哪天在大屏幕上看到你我一点儿都不会惊讶！

Dear Joyce,

I was rather impressed with the new packaging design you created for the skincare line. The gradient between blue and green along the edges is subtle but effective, and the background image of the snowcaps is refreshing. I'm confident that this will give us the competitive boost we need. Excellent job!

Cordially,

Martha

你为护肤品设计的新包装令我印象相当深刻。蓝边和绿边中间的斜线若隐若现但很有效果，后面山峰积雪的背景图案也让人耳目一新。我相信这会大大增强我们的竞争力。干得出色！

36 自信 Self-confidence

❶ I'm optimistic that we can finish the report on time. 　我很乐观我们会按时完成报告的。

❷ I'm sure that the product launch will be a complete success. 　我相信产品发布会会取得圆满成功。

❸ I'm confident that he'll decide to renew his contract with us. 　我相信他会再与我们联系的。

❹ I have every confidence that we'll be able to persuade her. 　我很有信心我们能说服她。

⑤ I have no doubt that our team will win Friday's basketball game.

毫无疑问周五的篮球比赛我们队一定会赢。

⑥ I know I have the ability to resolve this situation.

我知道我有解决这个状况的能力。

信例 1（生活类）

Hi Todd,

I've been busy writing and rewriting my valedictorian speech all week, and I'm finally satisfied with it. All that remains is to memorize it, which will only take a day or two at most. I'm sure I'll be in good shape to deliver the address at Monday's grad ceremony. How are things at your end?

Best regards,

Miriam

这一周我一直在忙着写我的告别演说词，我改了一遍又一遍，现在终于满意了。剩下的就是背下来，最多需要一两天。我相信在周一的毕业典礼上我一定能状态良好地发表演说。你那边事情怎么样？

信例 2（商务类）

Dear Aaron,

Have you read the market analysis for Southeast Asia yet? I just finished reviewing it. I'm confident that we can expand our market, especially in Malaysia and Singapore. If we move quickly, we should be able to gain substantial market share. At any rate, we can discuss this in further detail tomorrow morning.

Regards,

Raymond

你看了西南亚地区的市场分析了吗？我刚刚看完了，我对开拓我们的市场很有信心，尤其是马来西亚和新加坡的市场。如果我们动手快的话，我们应该能得到很大的市场份额。不管怎么说，我们明天早上再具体讨论一下这个问题。

---

37 鼓励 Encouragement

❶ You should believe in yourself.　　　你应该相信自己。

❷ You're doing a fine job.　　　你做得很好。

❸ We're all very proud of you.　　　我们都为你骄傲。

④ You did better than anyone I know. 　你做得比我认识的任何人都好。

⑤ You can accomplish any goal to which you aspire. 　你能够实现你想达到的任何目标。

⑥ I have total/complete confidence in you. 　我对你完全有信心。

⑦ I couldn't do even half as well as you. 　我连你的一半都赶不上。

⑧ There's no question that you will succeed. 　毫无疑问，你一定会成功的。

⑨ You've made amazing/unbelievable progress. 　你有了惊人的/难以想象的进步。

⑩ The most important thing is to never give up. 　最重要的事情是永不放弃。

⑪ I'm confident that your efforts will be rewarded. 　我相信你的努力一定会有回报的。

⑫ I'm sure you'll find a way to solve this problem. 　我相信你能找到办法解决这个问题。

⑬ You have my unconditional support. 　我全力以赴地支持你。

⑭ Keep up the good/excellent work! 　继续好好工作/出色完成工作！

⑮ I think you should go for it. 　我想你应该继续努力。

⑯ It doesn't hurt to try. 　尝试一下没什么害处。

⑰ Failures pave the road to success. 　失败是成功的必经之路。

⑱ I know you'll do even better next time. 　我知道你下次会做得更好。

⑲ You have a bright career ahead of you. 　你有着光明的前程。

⑳ Don't be discouraged by minor setbacks. 　不要遇到小困难就气馁。

㉑ Everyone encounters obstacles now and then. 　人有时会遇到困难。

㉒ Everything is going to turn out just fine. 　一切会好起来的。

㉓ Where there's a will, there's a way. 　有志者事竟成。

㉔ Things have a way of working out. 　事情会有解决办法的。

㉕ You should pursue your dreams. 　你应该追寻你的梦想。

㉖ Don't let anyone dissuade you. 　不要让任何人劝阻你。

信例1（生活类）

Dear Eva,

I know you're upset about your economics midterm. But there's really no need to worry about one bad grade. You still have two more years left until graduation, and your overall GPA is really all that matters. Besides, you're doing well in all your other courses, aren't you? Keep up your efforts and stay positive.

Best wishes,

Andrea

我知道你现在对经济学期中考试很不安，可是你真的没有必要担心成绩不好。你还有两年多才毕业呢，你的总成绩才是关键。再者说，你的其他科目成绩都很好，对吧？继续努力，保持积极状态。

信例2（商务类）

Hey Andy,

How on earth did you manage to sell four cars in your first week? I've been with the dealership for almost a year and it's the first time I've seen a rookie make so many deals so quickly. You have a promising sales career ahead of you. Keep up the good work!

Respectfully,

Jonathan

你到底是怎么在一周之内卖掉了四辆车的呢？我做销售都快一年了，这是我第一次看见新手能这么快就做成这么多笔交易的。你干销售这一行很有前途啊。继续好好干吧！

38 关心 Caring and concern

❶ Are you feeling any better? 　　　　　你感觉好些了吗？

❷ I hope you're feeling better soon. 　　我希望你尽快好起来。

❸ I haven't heard from you in a while. 　我好长时间没收到你的来信了。

❹ Have you been getting enough sleep? 　你最近睡眠充足吗？

❺ Make sure you get enough sleep. 　　你一定要有充足的睡眠。

❻ You must be tired after such a long flight. 　经过这么长时间的飞行，你一定累了。

❼ Have you adjusted to life in Denmark? 你习惯丹麦的生活了吗？

❽ I'm sure you'll find a new job soon. 我相信你不久就会找到一份新工作。

❾ How is your new job going? 你的新工作怎么样？

❿ How has work been going lately? 最近工作怎么样？

⓫ Let's go out this weekend to take your mind off the exam. 我们周末出去吧，散散心，把考试忘掉。

⓬ I hope you're finding time to get some exercise. 我希望你找时间做些锻炼。

⓭ I know how much stress you've been under recently. 我知道你最近一直压力极大。

⓮ How are your parents doing? 你的父母好吗？

⓯ I hope you'll be careful when you travel. 我希望你旅游的时候要小心。

⓰ Just let me know if there's anything I can do for you. 如果有什么需要我帮你做的尽管告诉我。

⓱ Is there anything I can help you with? 有什么我能帮你的吗？

⓲ I know it's not an easy situation to be in. 我知道进入状态不是很容易。

⓳ Try not to worry too much, okay? 别太担心了，好吗？

⓴ Try to keep your spirits up. 高兴点儿。

信例 1（生活类）

Hi Sophie,

It's too bad that things didn't work out between you and Dylan. But in reality, it was probably for the best … the two of you spent most of your time together arguing. Anyway, I know you'll find a new guy soon. As you always tell me, there are plenty of fish in the sea!

Take care,

Rebecca

你和迪伦还是分手了，挺让人痛心的。但是事实上，这也可能是件好事，因为你们两个在一起大部分时间都在吵架。不管怎么样，我知道你很快就会找到其他小伙子的。就像你常告诉我的，机会很多。

信例2（商务类）

Dear Jeff,

Stacy told me that you were out with the flu. I know you don't like missing work, but health is the number one priority. I can cover for you for a few days, so don't rush back into the office, alright? Remember to drink lots of fluids and get plenty of rest.

Best wishes,

Candace

丝塔茜告诉我你感冒了没来上班。我知道你不愿意放下工作。但是身体是第一位的。我给你几天假，你不用急着回来上班，好吗？记着要多喝水、多休息。

39 后悔 Regret

① I should have at least tried. 我本该至少试一试。

② I should have started studying earlier. 我本该再早点儿开始学习。

③ I ought to have known better. 我本应该多了解一些。

④ I shouldn't have made that comment. 我本不该作那样的评论。

⑤ I shouldn't have done that. 我本不该做这事。

⑥ I shouldn't have bought that stock. 我本不该买股票。

⑦ I know it was a mistake. 我知道这错了。

⑧ It's a pity that I didn't continue my piano lessons. 很遗憾我没能继续上我的钢琴课。

⑨ Looking back, I probably shouldn't have told him. 回过头想想，我真不该告诉他。

⑩ I'm filled with regret about what I said to her. 对于跟她说的话，我后悔极了。

⑪ I wish I could go back in time and start over. 希望我能及时回头，重新开始。

⑫ I wish I hadn't dropped out of college. 我多希望我没有被学校开除。

⑬ I can't believe I actually said that. 我真不相信我说了这话。

⑭ What was I thinking? 我一直都在想什么呢？

⑮ I wish I had done it differently. 我真希望我不是这么做的。

⑯ I feel ashamed of myself. 我真为自己感到惭愧。

Hi Vicky,

I really regret having gotten so upset with Donna yesterday. Considering that she's younger than me, I ought to be more tolerant and forgiving. Plus, she'll be my roommate for the rest of the year ... I hope I can still patch things up with her. How do you maintain such good relations with your roommate?

Yours,

Caroline

我真后悔昨天和唐娜闹得很不高兴。想想她比我小，我应该宽容些、谦让些。再说，这剩下的一年她还是我的室友。我希望能与她和好如初。你是怎么处理好与室友的关系的呢？

Dear Susan,

I know it was a big mistake to miss this morning's meeting. I missed the last one, too! This really wasn't the impression I was hoping to create. Did the boss say anything about my absence? I guess I'll have to think of a way to earn back some Brownie points....

See you at lunch,

Janice

我知道我又犯了个大错误，今天早晨的会议我没来。这是最后一次会议，我又缺席了。我真不是有意要给大家这样的印象。老板看我没来说什么了吗？我想我得想个办法讨回老板的欢心……

㊵ 生气 Anger

❶ I think you owe me an apology.   我想你应该向我道歉。

❷ I'm very upset with you right now.   我现在对你很生气。

❸ He often gets angry with his children.   他常跟孩子们发脾气。

❹ She's still upset at me for breaking her vase.   因为我打碎了她的花瓶，她还在跟我生气。

❺ It infuriates me to see your boss treating you this way.   看你老板这样对你让我很气愤。

❻ It angers me when I see people throwing away good food.   我看见有人把好好的食物扔掉就很生气。

⑦ It upsets me when you make derogatory comments about others.

你诋毁别人让我很气愤。

⑧ I'm frustrated by your lack of commitment.

你缺乏责任感让我很伤心。

⑨ I'm extremely upset at you for failing to keep your promise.

你食言让我非常气愤。

⑩ Your behavior at the party last night was unacceptable.

你昨天晚会上的表现让我无法接受。

⑪ I cannot begin to tell you how angry I am with you.

我说不出来我对你有多生气。

⑫ I'm extremely displeased with the author's biased points of view.

我对作者的偏见感到非常不满。

⑬ If you're late for another meeting, the boss is going to get really mad.

如果你开会再迟到的话，老板真的会生气了。

⑭ His indifferent attitude towards life makes me upset.

他对生活漠然的态度让我很不安。

⑮ Her lack of respect for elders is what angers me the most.

她对老人不尊重是最让我生气的了。

⑯ It makes my blood boil when people cut in front of me in line.

有人在我前面插队让我很生气。

⑰ I will not tolerate such unfounded criticisms.

我可受不了这种毫无理由的批评。

⑱ Do you think Alva is still upset with me?

你觉得阿尔瓦还在生我的气吗？

⑲ He has a bad/nasty/violent temper.

他脾气不好/恶劣/暴躁。

⑳ She frequently loses her temper.

她经常发脾气。

信例 1（生活类）

Hi Robert,

I can't tell you how angry I am with you. You were the one who offered to come over last night to help finish our assignment, and I was counting on you. By the time you finally e-mailed me this morning, I'd already handed it in. This isn't what I expected from you.

Winnie

我对你太气愤了。昨晚我找你过来帮我完成作业，我就指望你了，可你直到今早才发给我邮件，我都已经交完了。我真是指望不上你。

信例 2（商务类）

To Whom It May Concern,

I'm extremely upset with the poor service that I've received from your company. When I called yesterday, I had to wait almost an hour to speak to one of your representatives, and she barely even attempted to solve my problem. This kind of blatant disregard for your customers is inexcusable.

Sincerely,

Gordon Lewis

你们公司服务太差，太让我气愤了。昨天我打电话过来，我等了差不多一个小时才与你们的代表通话，而且她甚至根本就不想解决我的问题。你们对客户的不尊重实在不可原谅。

41 担心 Worry

❶ I'm worried that we might not finish the project on time.　我担心我们可能无法按时完成项目。

❷ I'm worried about Benny's health.　我担心班尼的健康。

❸ He always worries about what others might think of him.　他总是在意别人怎么想他。

❹ She worries constantly about her children's grades at school.　她总是担心她的孩子在学校的成绩。

❺ I'm feeling anxious about tomorrow's midterm exam.　我很担心明天的期中考试。

❻ I'm feeling uneasy about Monday's job interview.　周一的面试让我坐立不安。

❼ I often lose sleep worrying about my career prospects.　一想到我的工作前景我就失眠。

信例 1（生活类）

Hi Henry,

Did you hear about yesterday's market downturn in Tokyo and Hong Kong? I just bought a few tech stocks on the NYSE, and I'm worried that they might be influenced by the bad news in Asia. I know you do a lot of trading ... do you think you could give me some tips?

Regards,

Elisa

你听说昨天东京和香港股市低迷的消息了吗？我刚刚在纽约证券交易所买了几支科技股，我很担心它们会受到亚洲不好消息的影响。我知道你做过许多交易，你能给我些建议吗？

信例2（商务类）

Dear Bridget,

I'm worried that the client isn't going to be persuaded by our presentation. We're not their only potential supplier, and the competition we're up against is fierce. Could we meet at 7:30 am tomorrow to run through the presentation one more time? It wouldn't be too late to make any changes, if necessary.

Regards,

Christopher

我很担心我们的介绍不能说动客户，我们不是他们唯一的潜在供应商，而且我们面临的竞争相当激烈。我们明早 7 点半见个面，再看一遍我们的介绍，可以吗？如果有必要的话，现在做些改动还来得及。

42 害怕 Fear

❶ I fear that I'm going to lose my job. 　　我害怕我会失去工作。

❷ I've always had a fear of flying. 　　我一直害怕坐飞机。

❸ Even the thought of speaking in public makes me nervous. 　　甚至一想到在公众面前讲话我就紧张。

❹ I'm scared to walk alone at night in my neighborhood. 　　我害怕晚上一个人在小区里走。

❺ Six months after my house was robbed, I still live in constant fear. 　　我的房子被人偷窃后都 6 个月了，现在我还是一直后怕。

❻ He suffers from arachnophobia. 　　他患了恐惧症。

❼ She's absolutely terrified of snakes. 　　她太怕蛇了。

信例1（生活类）

Hey Karla,

I'm leaving this weekend for Germany to see my cousin, but I'm terrified of flying! The last time I set foot on a plane, I had to disembark before take-off and it was a total embarrassment. I remember you said that you used to have a fear of flying. How did you get over it?

Best regards,

Natasha

这周末我就要前往德国看望我表弟去了，但是我害怕坐飞机。上次我都上了飞机了，可是在起飞前我还是下去了，非常尴尬。我记得你说过你过去也害怕坐飞机，你是怎样克服的？

Hi Michael,

I'm feeling kind of nervous about my future with the company. Last week's layoffs were probably just the beginning ... and as a low-skilled worker, I'm in a vulnerable position. You're one of the company's rising stars, so you don't have anything to worry about. Do you think it's too late for me to upgrade my skills?

Regards,

Irena

我现在有点儿担心我在公司的前途。上周就开始裁员了，我是低技术工人，工作难保。你是公司的后起之秀，没有什么可担心的。你觉得我现在提高技能还来得及吗？

第六部分　论证观点
Expounding Arguments

43 例证 Examples and instances

❶ These examples underscore the importance of education in our society.

这些例子强调了教育在社会中的重要性。

❷ The speaker's arguments were supported by real-life examples.

活生生的例子可以证明演讲者的观点。

❸ Let me give you a few examples.

让我给你举几个例子。

❹ Could you give me some more/additional examples?

你能再给我举几个例子吗？

❺ China and India are the only two countries with populations exceeding one billion.

中国和印度是仅有的两个人口超过十亿的国家。

❻ Dwight was one of the few students who passed the final exam.

德怀特是少数几个期末考试及格的学生。

❼ I respect Carrie for her honesty, kindness and morality.

我敬佩卡丽的诚实、善良、讲道理。

❽ Cantonese, Shanghainese and Hakka are examples of Chinese dialects.

广东话、上海话、客家话都是中国方言的例子。

信例1（生活类）

Hi Marcy,

Guess what? Lucille and I started taking yoga classes at the community center yesterday. I hadn't realized all the benefits yoga offers.... Just to name a few, it can help to relieve stress, improve mental clarity, and increase flexibility and balance. The next class is on Thursday. Will you go with us?

Kindest regards,

Sandra

你猜怎么着？我和露西尔昨天在社区中心开始上瑜伽课了。我以前从来没意识到瑜伽能够带来这么多好处。比如说，它可以帮助减轻压力，使头脑清楚，提高柔韧性和平衡性。下次课是周二上，你愿意和我们一起去吗？

Dear Anne,

You asked me yesterday for pointers on how to design a website for your business. Basically, an effective website should be user-friendly, professional, and well-organized. In addition, the site's layout should be consistent, and content should be relevant and accurate. If your website possesses these characteristics, it'll have a chance at success.

Best of luck,

Darrell

你昨天问我怎样设计你们公司的网站。一个好的网站基本上应该是操作方便、专业性强而且结构合理。另外，网站的版式设计要连贯，内容要相关而且准确。如果你们的网站具备了这些特征，那就很有可能成功。

44 分类 Categorization

❶ Could you sort the client files alphabetically?

你能将客户档案按字母顺序分类吗？

❷ Do you consider yourself introverted or extroverted?

你觉得你自己是内向还是外向呢？

❸ I'm not sure whether to classify this movie as a drama or a comedy.

我不确定应该把这个电影归类到戏剧还是喜剧。

❹ I've sorted all my books into two broad categories—fiction and nonfiction.

我把我所有的书都归为两大类：小说和非小说。

❺ Be sure to divide your research sources into primary and secondary sources.

一定要把你的研究资料分成主要资料和次要资料。

❻ Internet security threats are categorized by level of danger.

互联网安全威胁要按危险的等级分类。

❼ The teacher placed the boys in one group and the girls in another.

老师把男孩分为一组、女孩分为一组。

❽ Based on his weight, he was placed in the featherweight boxing class.

根据他的体重，他被分到了次轻量级的拳击级别。

❾ Her illness was classified as severe and contagious.

她的病被断定为重病和传染病。

❿ It's important that you prioritize your work.

你能把工作按优先次序划分好很重要。

信例1（生活类）

Dear Students,

This is a reminder to include a bibliography with next week's term paper. You are required to divide the bibliography into two sections: primary and secondary sources. Primary sources include diaries, letters, speeches, interviews, autobiographies, and manuscripts. Secondary sources include textbooks, encyclopedias, reviews, and books that interpret previous research work.

Sincerely,

Judy Wilson

我想提醒大家下周交的学期论文要含有参考书目，你们要把参考书目分成两部分：主要资料和次要资料。主要资料包括日记、信函、演讲、采访、自传和手稿；次要资料包括教科书、百科全书、评论和能够解释前一阶段研究成果的书籍。

信例2（商务类）

Dear Harry,

There's a stack of client folders on the table in the printer room. If you have time either today or tomorrow, please separate them according to their status (i.e., active or inactive) and alphabetize them. The secretary will put them back in the filing cabinet when you're finished. Thanks very much.

Best regards,

Jennifer

打印室桌子上有一堆客户文件夹。如果你今天或者明天有时间的话，请根据客户的状况(即活跃的或不活跃的)把他们区分开，并按字母顺序排好。等你整理好了，秘书会把它们放入档案柜。多谢。

45　比较和对比 Comparison and contrast

❶ He's smarter than all the other children in his class.　他比他们班其他同学都聪明。

❷ She's more mature than most other kids of her age.　她比同龄的其他小孩都成熟。

❸ Edward speaks Japanese just as well as Freda.　爱德华和弗雷达的日语说得一样好。

④ I didn't like his latest novel as much as his previous one. 我不像喜欢他前一本小说那样喜欢这本最新的。

⑤ I think my arguments were more persuasive than hers. 我觉得我的观点比她的更有说服力。

⑥ You're more experienced in these matters than I am. 你在这些事情上比我更有经验。

⑦ We have to choose the best of the proposed solutions. 我们要从提议的解决方案中挑出最好的。

⑧ The Chinese runner beat the previous record by 0.15 seconds. 中国赛跑者以 0.15 秒之差打破了之前的记录。

⑨ Is it true that strawberries are richer in vitamin C than oranges? 草莓比桔子富含维生素 C，这是真的吗?

⑩ He's taller and stronger than most of his classmates. 他比他们班所有男生都高大、强壮。

⑪ She's much more computer-savvy than her colleagues. 她比她的同事更懂计算机。

⑫ Sichuan cuisine is generally spicier than Cantonese food. 一般说来，川菜比粤菜要辣。

⑬ I believe that the present is more important than the past. 我觉得现在比过去要重要得多。

⑭ I think that love and friendship are more important than money. 我认为爱情和友谊比金钱更重要。

⑮ There's a sharp contrast between the writing styles of Ba Jin and Lu Xun. 巴金和鲁迅的写作风格有着天壤之别。

⑯ The tallest NBA player is over 50 centimeters taller than the shortest one. 最高的 NBA 球员比最矮的要高 50 公分。

⑰ Greg and Henry are really different, so it's hard to compare them. 格雷格和亨利截然不同，所以很难把他们作比较。

⑱ There's a large gap between the two countries' populations. 这两个国家的人口差距很大。

⑲ His personality changed abruptly following the tragedy. 看完这个悲剧，他的个性突然改变了。

⑳ Her studies have improved dramatically this year. 今年她的学习有了很大提高。

信例1（生活类）

Hey Emma,

Have you talked to Marge recently? I heard she was cut from the track-and-field team for missing too many practices. It's surprising, because she was faster than any of the other runners. If the coach had an issue with her attendance, he could have at least given her a warning. Hope she's doing alright.

See you tomorrow,

Britney

最近你和玛吉谈过吗？我听说她因为缺了许多次训练，被田径队刷下来了。太让人惊讶了，因为她比其他队员跑得都快。如果教练不满意她的出勤的话，他本可以至少给她一次警告嘛。希望她一切顺利。

信例2（商务类）

Dear Ross,

I've calculated the written test scores for the remaining candidates. Ethan received 95 points, the highest score in the group. Diana came in a close second with 90 points, and Trish ranked third with 75 points. Kenny's score fell below the cutoff line. Please refer to the attachment for a detailed breakdown.

Best regards,

Janet

我已经计算出剩下的报考者的写作成绩。伊桑 95 分，是这一组的最高分。戴安娜 90 分位居第二，特里诗 75 分位居第三。肯尼的分数低于录取线。详细分类，请查看附件。

46 概括 Summarization

❶ To sum up, my new job is difficult but equally rewarding.　　总而言之，我的新工作很有难度但是报酬也很多。

❷ He briefly summarized the company's aims.　　他简要地概括了公司未来的目标。

❸ She gave a summary of her views on education.　　她概括了对教育的观点。

❹ Can you help me write an abstract for my article?

你能帮我写一篇我论文的摘要吗?

❺ The brochure should include an outline of our company's history.

宣传手册应该包括我们公司的历史概况。

❻ The book condenses over 5,000 years of Chinese history into about 200 pages.

这本书把五千多年的中国历史缩成了 200 页左右。

❼ Let me tell you briefly what happened.

我给你简单讲讲事情的经过。

❽ I have to write an overview of the week's news for my journalism class.

我得为新闻课写一篇对这一周新闻的概述。

❾ I like reading the abridged versions of really long novels.

我喜欢读长篇小说的节本。

信例 1(生活类)

Hi Paula,

Just a short note to tell you that I passed my driving test! In short, I had to make a three-point turn, drive on the highway for a few minutes, make an emergency stop, and finally reverse park. The test wasn't really as hard as I'd expected. How have your driving lessons been going?

Kind regards,

Malcolm

我只想告诉你我通过驾驶测试了。简言之,我必须做三点掉头、在高速路上开几分钟、急刹车、最后倒车停车。考试没有我想象得那么难。你的驾驶课程怎么样了?

信例 2(商务类)

Dear Vince,

I looked at your draft of the brochure text this morning, and I think we should try to condense it. For each section, let's keep the word count below 100 words. That way, we'll be able to increase the font size and add a few more images. Please e-mail me the revised copy by tomorrow.

Best regards,

Kirsten

你好,今天早上我看了你写的宣册手册的草稿,我觉得我们应该压缩一下内容。每一部分的字数都控制在一百字以内。那样我们就能加大字号,还可以添加几张图片。明天你把修改过的文件发给我一份。

47 推断 Inferences

❶ I gathered from his silence that he's unwilling to accept the agreement.

我从他的沉默看出来他不愿意接受这个协议。

❷ Her position on this issue can be inferred from recent comments she made.

她在这个问题上的立场能够从她最近做的评论中推断出来。

❸ Given his performance on the final exam, it's unlikely that he'll pass the course.

鉴于他在期末考试中的表现，他不大可能通过考试。

❹ The doctor inferred that Ian's lung cancer was caused by years of heavy smoking.

医生推断说伊恩的肺癌是多年过量吸烟造成的。

❺ From the data, he extrapolated that the world population would surpass 10 billion by 2050.

他从数据上推论出到 2050 年世界人口会超过一百亿。

❻ Judging by the client's last e-mail, it would appear that they're pleased with our work.

从客户的上一封电子邮件看出，他们对我们的工作非常满意。

❼ It's reasonable to say that poor eating habits have contributed to Jill's obesity.

不好的饮食习惯导致了吉尔的肥胖，这话很有道理。

❽ Based on the evidence, the jury reasoned that he was guilty of all charges.

依据事实，法官得出结论他对所有指控都有罪。

❾ I gathered from her body language that she was feeling uncomfortable.

我从她的肢体语言猜出她感觉不舒服。

信例 1（生活类）

Hey Gail,

I talked to Katie last night, and it's pretty evident that she's having relationship problems with Josh. Whenever she's really quiet on the phone, like she was last night, it's usually a sign of boyfriend trouble. Do you think we should take her out this weekend? It'd probably help cheer her up.

Yours truly,

Claudia

我昨晚和卡蒂谈了，很明显她和乔希之间的关系出问题了。每次要是她在电话里沉默寡言的话，就像昨晚那样，十有八九就是和男朋友闹别扭了。你觉得我们应不应该周末叫她出去玩儿，可能会使她高兴点儿。

Dear Alan,

Have you looked at the latest sales data? Our sales this quarter were down almost 10 percent from the same period last year, despite significantly increasing our advertising expenditures. And the overall economy is in good shape. I think it's safe to say that the competition is heating up, wouldn't you agree?

Regards,

Danielle

你看了最新的销售数据了吗？尽管我们广告的花销急剧增长，可是这个季度我们的销售同比下降了十个百分点。总体经济状况还是挺好的。我可以有把握地说竞争越来越白炽化了，你觉得呢？

48 阐明 Elucidation

❶ I would like you to define and elucidate the key issues in your report.

我希望你能在报告中详细阐明关键问题。

❷ The professor explained everything slowly to make sure we all understood.

教授慢慢地解释了所有的问题，以确保我们都能够明白。

❸ In his speech, the CEO expounded his company's position on sustainable energy.

首席执行官在他的演讲中阐述了公司在可持续能源上的立场。

❹ In her new book, the author clarified her position on the issue of global warming.

在这本新书里，作者阐明了她对全球变暖问题的立场。

❺ Could you explain what the investment terms "selling short" and "going long" mean?

你能解释投资术语"selling short"和"going long"的意思吗？

❻ He gave the police a detailed account of what he remembered from that night.

他对警察详细描述了他记起来的那天晚上发生的事情。

❼ She gave me a list of the reasons why she turned down the job offer.

她告诉我许多她拒绝这份工作的原因。

❽ I'm impressed at how clearly and thoroughly Kara expressed her plan.

凯拉特别清楚透彻地表达了她的想法，给我留下深刻印象。

Hey Alicia,

Did you understand the economics lecture this morning? I know the prof was trying to explain the relationship between scarcity and opportunity costs ... but to tell you the truth, most of it went over my head. If you're not doing anything tomorrow, let's study together for next week's quiz. I'll call you later tonight.

Yours,

Larissa

你明白今天上午经济学课讲的内容了吗？我知道教授一直在解释短缺和机会成本之间的关系……但是说实话，大部分内容都太深奥了，我听不懂。如果你明天没什么事的话，我们一起学习准备下周的测验吧。晚上我给你打电话。

Hi Stan,

I took the morning off to see my doctor, and he said that my lack of exercise is impairing my health. He explained that if I don't increase my level of physical activity, I could even be at risk for heart disease. If you don't mind, I think I'll join you at the gym after work.

Regards,

Ernest

我上午请假去看医生了，他说我缺乏锻炼所以体质越来越差，他解释说如果我不加强体能锻炼的话，有可能会得心脏病。如果你不介意的话，我想下班后跟你去健身房。

49 结论 Conclusions

❶ I've concluded that learning a foreign language is no easy task.　　我觉得学习一门外语不是件容易的事情。

❷ The study concluded that stress contributes to heart disease.　　研究表明压力可以导致心脏病。

❸ The scientists concluded that an epidemic is likely in the next five years.　　科学家认为在未来五年可能会爆发流行病。

④ I believe that the researchers were erroneous in their conclusion.

我觉得研究人员的结论是错误的。

⑤ The doctor reached the conclusion that further treatment would be futile.

医生得出结论：进一步的治疗是无效的。

⑥ The conclusions made by the two authors were surprisingly similar.

两位作家的结论惊人地相似。

⑦ Make sure that your conclusions are clearly stated in the abstract.

一定要使你的结论在摘要中清晰地表述出来。

⑧ I'm not sure whether your report's conclusions are convincing.

我不确定你报告的结论是否很有说服力。

信例 1（生活类）

Hi Lynn,

Well, I finally decided to take your advice and have a home security system installed. After considering all the variables that you mentioned and doing my own research, I concluded that it's indeed a worthwhile investment. You were right when you said that peace of mind is what matters the most.

All the best,

Donnie

我最终决定听取你的建议，安装家庭安全系统。考虑了你提到的所有可能性，和我自己做的调查，我觉得这确实是值得的投资。你说得对，心境的平静才是最重要的。

信例 2（商务类）

Dear Ryan,

Has the quality control team concluded the cause of the sudden increase in product defects? Please check on their progress. As you're aware, production will remain on hold until we're able to determine what the problem is and resolve it. I would like to see production back on line before the next shift.

Sincerely,

Blake Moore

质检小组找出产品瑕疵突然上升的原因了吗？请查看他们的进展情况。正如你所注意到的，我们必须找到问题所在，并且能够解决它，否则的话生产就会陷入停滞状态。我希望产品在下次换班之前能恢复生产。

第七部分 说明时间
Describing Time

50 时刻 Time

❶ I have classes every day from 8:00 to 11:30 am.

我每天从上午 8 点到中午 11 点半上课。

❷ I heard your flight was delayed by over 5 hours.

我听说你的飞机晚点了 5 个多小时。

❸ I have to get up at 6:30 tomorrow morning.

明天早上我得 6 点半起床。

❹ If we leave at 7:45, we should be able to get there by 8:30.

如果我们 7:45 出发，我们应该能在 8:30 之前到那儿。

❺ The school year begins in September and ends in June.

学校 9 月份开学，6 月份放假。

❻ He's moving into a new apartment next week.

他下周要搬进新公寓。

❼ She has to submit her dissertation by next Friday.

她下周五得上交学位论文。

❽ The best time to take action is right now.

现在是采取行动的最佳时机。

❾ My job interview is this Monday at 2:30 pm.

我的工作面试是这周一下午两点半。

信例 1（生活类）

Hi Ian,

How's your day going so far? Mine's been a bit hectic. I met with a client this morning, and I still have two meetings lined up this afternoon. By the way, we're still meeting for coffee tonight, right? Shall I pick you up at 8:00? I'll call you after work to confirm.

Regards,

Erica

最近过得怎么样？我最近有点儿忙。今天上午我见了一个客户，下午还有两个会。顺便问一下，今晚我们还是去喝咖啡，对吧？我 8 点去接你怎么样？下班后我打电话跟你确认。

Dear Rosemary,

Would it be possible to schedule my remaining vacation days this year for the first week in August? Or, if those days are unavailable, the last week in August would also be fine. I'm planning to take my wife and kids to New Zealand this summer. Thanks in advance.

Best regards,

Shawn Collins

我可以在 8 月的第一周休我今年剩余的假期吗？如果那几天不行的话，8 月的最后一周也可以。我想这个夏天带我的爱人和孩子去新西兰。我在这里先谢谢了。

51 频度 Frequency

❶ I type about 100 to 120 words per minute. 　　我每分钟能打 100 到 120 个字。

❷ I usually check my e-mail about five times a day. 　　我通常一天要查看 5 次电子邮件。

❸ They visit their relatives in the Netherlands every summer. 　　他们每年夏天都去探望在荷兰的亲戚。

❹ The doctor said I should take the medicine twice a day. 　　医生说这个药我应该一天吃两次。

❺ My dad and I usually e-mail each other once a week. 　　我和爸爸每周通一封电子邮件。

❻ He frequently goes to Europe on business trips. 　　他经常去欧洲出差。

❼ She is a regular customer of our store. 　　她是我们商店的常客。

❽ We play tennis two or three times a week. 　　我们每周打两三次网球。

信例1（生活类）

Hey Amy,

I decided that I want to lose some weight, so I've begun planning an exercise regimen. Starting next week, I'm going to go jogging every morning, take an aerobics class on Tuesdays, and go for a swim at least twice a week. Are you interested in joining me? It'd be a lot more fun together.

Yours,

Debbie

我想减肥，因此计划先从运动常规训练开始。从下周起，我打算每天早上都去慢跑，周二跳有氧健身操，每周至少再游两次泳。你有兴趣跟我一起练吗？两个人一起锻炼一定会有趣得多。

信例2（商务类）

Dear Al,

We've had frequent complaints in the past few days from customers unable to access our website. Our new webmaster, Naomi Ward, is on vacation until tomorrow, so I want you to look into this issue in the meantime. Please make this a priority and drop any other work you have for the time being.

Regards,

Eliot

前一段时间我们不断接到客户投诉说无法登陆咱们的网站。咱们的新网站主管纳奥米·沃德休假去了，后天才来上班。希望你现在能查一下到底是哪里出了问题。请先把手边的工作放下，集中精力解决这个问题。

52　时序和顺序 Sequence and order

❶ The client files should be sorted in alphabetical order.   客户档案应该按照字母顺序分类。

❷ I'll call you up tonight after I get home from the office.   我今晚下班回家之后给你打电话

❸ I'm giving the first of a series of presentations on Monday.   周一我要做系列演讲的第一场。

❹ We have to memorize the chronological order of the Chinese dynasties.   我们得把中国的各个朝代按时间顺序记住。

❺ Please list your choices according to preference, from most to least preferred.

请根据你的喜好程度由高到低列出选项。

❻ Larry finished the marathon first, followed by Marge and then Neil.

拉里率先跑完了马拉松，紧随其后的是玛吉，然后是尼尔。

❼ He talked about the phases of the product life cycle in yesterday's lecture.

他在昨天的讲座里讲到了产品生命周期的各个阶段。

❽ She developed a bad cold today after staying up late last night.

由于昨晚睡得太晚，今天她的感冒加重了。

❾ Heavy rain has been forecast for Friday, but Saturday is supposed to be sunny.

天气预报说周五有大雨，但周六会放晴。

❿ Let's play tennis tomorrow morning and go shopping in the afternoon.

咱们明天上午去打网球，下午去逛街吧。

⓫ The investigator asked me to recount the sequence of events of that day.

那位探员让我把那天发生的事按顺序再叙述一遍。

⓬ I want to get married when I'm 30 and have kids before I turn 32.

我打算 30 岁结婚，32 岁前生孩子。

⓭ I'll drop by your place tomorrow morning before school, okay?

我明早上学之前去你家找你，好吗？

⓮ I arrived at the airport an hour prior to my departure.

我到机场的时候离飞机起飞还有一小时。

信例1（生活类）

Hi Jill,
I checked the schedule for that new action movie being released today. There are shows playing tonight at the downtown cinema at 6:30, 7:20, 8:10, and 9:00. We should probably get there half an hour in advance to get tickets. I'll be out of the office by around 5:30 today … how about you?
See you soon,
Alvin

我查了影院的时间表，那部新动作片今天上映。市中心的电影院晚上 6:30、7:20、8:10 和 9:00 各演一场。咱们最好提前半小时去买票。我大概 5:30 左右从办公室出发……你呢？

Dear Walter,

The new product catalog hasn't been sent to the printer yet, has it? If it's not too late, I want to change the order in which the products are listed. Instead of ordering them alphabetically by product name, I'd like to have the products listed by price (from most to least expensive). Thanks in advance.

Regards,

Gail Parker

新产品目录还没有付印吧？如果还来得及的话，我想更改一下目录里的产品顺序。原来是按产品名字的首字母顺序排序的，现在想按照价格顺序重排(从高到低)。先谢了。

53 速度 Speed/Velocity

❶ I was driving at 125 km/h when the cop pulled me over. 　　警察让我把车开到路边的时候，我开车的时速达到了 125 公里。

❷ I felt that the movie's plot developed too slowly. 　　我觉得那部电影的剧情发展得太慢了。

❸ Owen can run 100 meters in under 12 seconds. 　　欧文百米能跑 12 秒以内。

❹ Paula is a fast learner and has made rapid progress at school this year. 　　保拉学得很快，这个学期进步非常迅速。

❺ The new high-speed train has a maximum speed of 600 km/h. 　　这种新型列车的最高时速可以达到 600 公里。

❻ One of my friends can read over 500 words a minute. 　　我有个朋友一分钟能看 500 个字。

❼ I'm still not used to the fast tempo of life in the big city. 　　我仍然不习惯这个大城市快速的生活节奏。

Hi Don,

How did you do on yesterday's Chinese test? Bruce managed to finish it in only an hour…. He must have answered the questions really fast. As for me, I barely finished. I'm a slow reader, so it took me forever to get through the reading comprehension passages. Anyhow, I hope we both did okay.

Kind regards,

Laurie

昨天的汉语考试你考得怎么样？布鲁斯只用了一个小时就答完了……他答题的速度肯定特别快。我就差点儿没答完。我的阅读速度很慢，所以做阅读理解题的时候总是要花很长时间。当然，无论如何希望咱们都能考得好。

Dear Ivan,

How is your development team progressing with the software patch? Since this is a high-risk security flaw, I want the patch released as soon as possible. If necessary, we can assign additional programmers to your team in order to expedite your progress. Let me know if you require any other resources.

Thanks,

Melinda

你们研发小组的软件补丁工作进行得如何了？鉴于原来存在着高危安全漏洞，我希望软件补丁能尽快发布。如果可以的话，我们还可以另外再给你们小组派一名程序员，帮助你尽快完成。如果你们还需要什么资源尽管跟我说。

54 同时 Simultaneity

❶ I was driving home when the plane crash occurred.   飞机失事的时候我正在开车回家。

❷ I've been multitasking a lot recently.   我最近要同时处理好几件事情。

❸ You need to consider both qualitative and quantitative factors.   质量和数量你都要兼顾。

❹ You shouldn't use your cell phone while driving.   开车的时候不要打手机。

❺ He finished all the popcorn during the movie.

看电影的时候他把爆米花都吃掉了。

❻ She usually stays at home while her husband is at work.

她丈夫上班的时候她总是待在家里。

❼ We need to finish both reports by the end of the day.

今天下班之前我们得把两份报告都写完。

❽ I can't believe I slept right through the earthquake.

我真不敢相信地震的时候我居然睡得很安稳。

信例 1（生活类）

Hi Rose,

I just looked at my schedule for tomorrow.... Somehow, I've got a tennis match and a chess tournament both scheduled for 2:00 pm. I can't be in two places at once, so I'll have to miss one of them. But I can't decide which one to give up. What's your opinion?

Yours truly,

Serena

我刚刚查了我明天的日程安排……到目前为止，我有一场网球比赛和一场象棋比赛都安排在下午两点了。我不可能同时出现在两个赛场上，所以肯定要放弃一个。不过我还没决定选哪一个。你觉得呢？

信例 2（商务类）

Dear Joey,

I know you're busy trying to finish the proposal before punching out, but I have one more thing to add to your to-do list. The file I'm attaching needs to be formatted before being e-mailed to the client by 6:00. If you can work to get both tasks done today, it would be tremendously appreciated.

Best regards,

Calvin

我知道你正忙着想在下班之前把计划书写完，不过还有一件事得麻烦你办。我手头上有一份文件需要排版，然后在 6 点以前发邮件给客户。如果这两件事你今天都能完成的话，就实在是太感谢了。

55 持续 Continuity

❶ I've been working as a legal advisor for 15 years.　我做了 15 年的法律顾问。

❷ He has accumulated considerable wealth over the years.　这些年来他攒了不少钱。

❸ She was elected to a second term as major.　她当选连任第二任市长。

❹ Half a year later, the police still have no clues in the murder case.　半年过去了，警察对这起谋杀案依然毫无头绪。

❺ You should persevere in pursuing your ambitions.　你应该为自己的理想坚持不懈地努力。

信例 1（生活类）

Hey Luke,

How've you been? I've been lying in bed for the past three days…. Anytime I get a bad cold, it always seems to persist for at least a week before I start to gradually feel better. Did I miss anything important in Wednesday's English lecture? Did the prof return our essays?

Best regards,

Estelle

你最近过得怎么样？我前一阵在床上足足躺了 3 天……我每次得重感冒都会难受一个星期，之后才能慢慢有些起色。这周三的英语课讲什么重要内容了吗？咱们的论文教授退回来了吗？

信例 2（商务类）

Dear Staff,

This is a reminder that our office's annual food drive begins tomorrow and will continue until the end of next week. All donations should be nonperishable items, including canned foods, dried noodles, peanut butter, cereals, and snacks. (See the attachment for a comprehensive list.) Thank you for your support.

Sincerely,

Jack Harris

提醒大家，从明天起我们部门一年一度的食物募捐活动就要开始了，活动将会一直持续到下周末。捐赠的食品必须是耐储存的，包括罐头、挂面、花生酱、麦片和零食。（详细内容请参见附件里的清单。）谢谢大家的支持。

第八部分　描述空间
Describing Space

56 位置 Position

❶ I usually like to sit near the front of the classroom.

我一般喜欢坐在教室的前面。

❷ A new movie theater is being built in my neighborhood.

我家附近新建了一座电影院。

❸ The exam will be held in Room 301 of Stephenson Hall.

考试地点是史蒂文森大楼 301 房间。

❹ I'll drop off the books in your mailbox tomorrow morning.

明天早上我会把那些书放在你的信箱里。

❺ The Forbidden City is located in the center of Beijing.

紫禁城位于北京的中心。

❻ We're planning to move downtown early next year.

我们打算明年年初搬到市中心去。

信例1（生活类）

Hi Fran,

Did you hear that there's going to be a new mall built across the street from our campus? It'll be nice to finally have easy access to restaurants, stores, coffee shops, and maybe even a cinema. I just hope it'll be finished soon, so we'll have a chance to enjoy it before we graduate.

Kind regards,

Rhonda

你听说了吗？咱们学校街对面新建的是一家购物中心。今后咱们吃饭、买东西、喝咖啡，甚至是看电影就都很方便了。真希望它能尽快建好，那么咱们在毕业之前还能尽情地享受一番。

Dear Walter,

There are some cardboard boxes on the table at the back of the mailroom. They should have been delivered to the fifth floor but were sent up to our office by mistake. If you're not too busy this morning, I would appreciate it if you could bring them downstairs to room 510.

Thanks,

Charlene

信件收发室靠里的桌子上有几个硬纸盒子。那些本来是应该送到 5 层的，结果错送到我们部门了。今天上午如果你有空的话，要是能帮我把这些盒子送到楼下的 510 室去就太感谢了。

57 方向 Direction

❶ I'm still trying to plan the route for our trip to Delaware.

我还在研究我们去特拉华州的路线。

❷ We're planning to drive from Kunming to Lijiang tomorrow.

我们正在计划明天从昆明开车去丽江。

❸ You can take the number 101 bus to the city center.

你可以坐 101 路汽车到市中心去。

❹ Just follow the attached directions and you'll be able to find the restaurant.

只要按照路线说明走，你就能找到那家餐厅。

❺ You should take a compass when you go hiking, just in case you get lost.

你去远足的时候最好带个指南针，以防迷路。

❻ He's going to bike from Calgary to Edmonton on Sunday.

他打算周日从卡尔加里骑车到埃德蒙顿。

❼ She has a horrible sense of direction and gets lost easily.

她的方向感特别差，很容易迷路。

信例1（生活类）

Hey Kayla,

We've decided to go to a restaurant called Pronto Steakhouse to celebrate Dale's birthday this weekend. The reservation is for Saturday night at 7:30. To get there from your area, you just need to drive north along Archer Street till you reach Baker Road, and it's on the southeast corner. See you there!

Warm regards,

Rosanne

我们决定这个周末去一家名叫"急速"的牛排馆庆祝黛尔的生日。已经订好了周六晚上7:30的位子。从你那儿过去应该沿着人马座大街向北开，一直到贝克路，饭馆就在那条路的东南角。咱们到那儿见吧！

信例2（商务类）

Dear Colleagues,

This year's holiday party will be held on December 15th at 7:00 pm. The venue will be Magnum Cafe, which is located three blocks west of Union Station (see the attached map for directions). We hope that everyone can attend. As always, please feel free to bring along your spouse or significant other.

Best wishes,

EricKing

今年的节日宴会将于12月15日晚上7:00举行。集合地点定在"两夸脱"咖啡店，位于联合车站向西三个街区（具体位置请见附件里的地图）。希望各位届时都来参加。并且和往届一样，欢迎大家自愿携伴侣出席。

58 距离 Distance

❶ I live roughly 25 kilometers from Tian'anmen Square.

我住的地方距天安门广场大约有25公里。

❷ We live about a 10-minute drive from each other.

我们两个住的地方相距大约开车10分钟的路程。

❸ The museum is about five kilometers away from the subway station.

那家博物馆距地铁站大约5公里远。

❹ There are several good restaurants within walking distance of my house. 　　我家附近有几家不错的饭馆，步行就能到。

❺ Shanghai and Beijing are separated by approximately 1,500 km. 　　上海和北京相距大约 1500 公里。

❻ It'll take us just over three hours to get there by train. 　　我们坐火车到那里去需要 3 个多小时。

信例 1（生活类）

Hey Zack,

I wanted to tell you that I got a new job! I'm going to be working evenings at an Italian restaurant downtown. The best part about it is that the restaurant is only a few miles from my house. My last job was in the suburbs and it took me ages to get there.

Keep in touch,

Marissa

告诉你我找到新工作啦！今后我晚上都将在市中心的一家意大利餐厅上班。最令人满意的是，那家餐厅离我家只有几英里远。我的上一份工作在郊区，路上要花很长时间才能到。

信例 2（商务类）

Hi Carmen,

Do you want to take part in the charity run on Saturday morning? I went last year and had a really good time. The course is only five miles long, and most runners are able to finish within an hour. Anyway, think about it and let me know tomorrow at work.

Best regards,

Heather

你想参加周六上午的慈善长跑吗？去年的这个活动我去了，感觉很不错。全程只有 5 英里，大部分人都能在 1 小时内跑完全程。你考虑考虑吧，明天上班的时候告诉我你的决定。

59 面积和体积 Area and volume

❶ We want to move into a more spacious apartment. 　　我们想要搬到一套更宽敞的公寓里去。

❷ The new golf resort covers more than 400 acres of land.

新高尔夫球场的占地面积是 400 多英亩。

❸ The Forbidden City covers an area of 720,000 square meters.

紫禁城的占地面积是 72 万平方米。

❹ Alaska has an area of more than half a million square miles.

阿拉斯加的总面积是 50 多万平方英里。

❺ His swimming pool can hold over 6,000 gallons of water.

他的游泳池可以容纳 6000 加仑的水。

❻ Her fish tank holds about five liters of water.

她的鱼缸能盛 5 升水。

❼ My coffee mug has a volume of 250 ml.

我的咖啡杯容积为 250 毫升。

信例 1（生活类）

Hey Wes,

I just found out about a new golf resort being built 120 kilometers north of the city. It's supposed to cover an area of more than 500 acres and will include three golf courses, indoor and outdoor tennis courts, and other recreational facilities. Do you want to check it out when it opens?

Cheers,

Nicholas

我最近发现市区往北 120 公里新开了一家高尔夫度假村。它的占地面积大约有 500 多英亩，里面有 3 个高尔夫球场、室内和室外的网球场以及一些其他的娱乐设施。那里正式营业后你想去看看吗？

信例 2（商务类）

Hi Jimmy,

I'm thinking about moving into a bigger apartment. As you know, my place is pretty small—the floor area's only around 500 sq ft. If you don't mind me asking, what's your condo's floor area? Is the rent steep? I want to find a place closer to our office if possible.

Best regards,

Chuck

我想搬到一套大一些的公寓里去。你知道的，我现在住的地方实在是太小了——总面积只有大约 500 平方英尺。如果你不介意的话，能告诉我你的公寓面积吗？房租是不是很贵啊？如果可以的话，我希望能找到一套离上班的地方近一些的房子。

第九部分　说明数量
Describing Quantity

60　数 Number

❶ The company has over 20,000 employees worldwide.

这家公司在全球有两万多名员工。

❷ There are about 25 students in my English class.

我的英语班大约有 25 个学生。

❸ Could you call the restaurant and make a reservation for 12 people?

你能打电话给那家餐厅预订 12 个人的座席吗?

❹ He has written three novels in the past two years.

在过去的两年间他写了三部小说。

❺ She has a collection of over 3,000 ancient coins.

她收集了 3000 多枚古代钱币。

❻ Please bring 500 copies of the handout to the conference.

请带 500 份材料来开会。

❼ The exam will consist of 50 multiple-choice questions.

这次考试将有 50 道多项选择题。

信例 1（生活类）

Hi Will,

It was really nice of you to offer to pick up supplies for the party. For drinks, I think we could use around 24 beers, two bottles of vodka, and three large colas. In terms of snacks, a few bags of potato chips ought to do it. We can order pizzas after everyone comes.

Thanks again,

Jerry

你愿意负责咱们这次聚会的饮食实在是太好了。酒水方面，我觉得大概需要 24 瓶啤酒、两瓶伏特加和三大瓶可乐。至于零食，几包薯片大概就够了。人到齐之后，咱们可以叫披萨外卖。

信例2（商务类）

Hey Chris,

How's it going? I stopped by that new gym near our office yesterday to take a look. The facilities are fairly complete: there are about 30 stationary bikes, 20 treadmills, 10 elliptical trainers, and lots of free weights and weight machines. Do you want to go for a workout together one day this week?
Lenny

最近过得怎么样？我昨天去咱们单位旁边新开的健身房看了看。里面的设施很齐全：有将近30部固定自行车、20部跑步机、10部椭圆运转机，还有许多自由调节重量的器材和举重器械。你想不想这周抽一天时间咱俩一起去试试？

61 量 Amount

❶ I've been spending a great deal of my time studying.　　我花了大量的时间用来学习。

❷ We've received multiple complaints from clients this week.　　这周我们收到了各种各样的客户投诉。

❸ He made sizable donations to several local charities.　　他对一些当地的慈善团体给予了大量的捐助。

❹ She has been eating less and less recently.　　她最近吃得越来越少了。

❺ The library has an extensive collection of audiovisual materials.　　这家图书馆有丰富的视听教材。

❻ It's been raining heavily all month here.　　这里整整一个月都在下大雨。

❼ Quincy read a stack of novels this past month.　　昆西上个月看了好多小说。

❽ I can't even count how many movies I saw last year.　　去年我看的电影简直数不胜数。

Hey Deb,

How was your holiday? Did you have fun in Jamaica? Most of my time was spent lying on the couch watching a bunch of movies. I also read a few novels. It was a relaxing two weeks, but kind of boring, too. I think I'll follow your example and go someplace warm next winter!

Best wishes,

Pauline

假期过得如何？在牙买加玩儿得开心吗？我这个假期大部分时间都窝在沙发里看了好多电影，还读了几本小说。这两周过得真舒服啊，不过也有点儿无聊。明年冬天我打算向你学习，也找个暖和的地方去玩一玩。

Dear Mr. Foster,

Since I'm already working on several projects, I don't think it would be realistic for me to take on another one at this time. Is there anyone else who could handle it? I'm just afraid that quality might be compromised if I take on too many tasks at once. Thank you for your understanding.

Sincerely,

Mindy Russell

鉴于我手里已经有好几个项目正在进行中，因此不太可能再接受其他项目了。还有其他可以处理这个问题的人选吗？如果要我同时管理太多项目，恐怕难以保证质量。谢谢您的理解。

62 足量和不足量 Sufficiency and insufficiency

❶ I think we have enough people to complete the project on time.

我觉得我们有足够的人手能按时完成这个工程。

❷ If we leave at 6:00 am, we should have ample time to get to the airport.

如果我们早上 6 点出发，那么肯定有充裕的时间去机场。

❸ Do we have enough food supplies for the party?

咱们为宴会准备的食物够吗？

4 I heard Ralph finally saved up enough money to buy his own airplane.

我听说拉尔夫总算攒够了钱去买一架私人飞机。

5 He's the only job candidate who possesses sufficient experience.

他是这个职位唯一有丰富工作经验的应聘者。

6 She's definitely attractive enough to be a runway model.

她绝对是一个极富吸引力的走台模特。

7 I haven't been getting enough sleep recently.

我最近睡眠不太够。

8 Saul seems to be lacking in responsibility.

索尔似乎缺乏责任感。

9 You'd better spend more time on your studies.

你最好多花些时间在学习上。

10 Inadequate rainfall has caused a decline in agricultural production.

雨水不足造成农作物减产。

11 We're still over $10,000 away from our fundraising target.

跟我们的筹款目标还差1万美元。

12 I don't think we have enough time left to finish the proposal.

我觉得想要完成这个计划我们时间不够。

信例1（生活类）

Hi Jim,

I'm wondering whether we have enough food for the camping trip. Maybe we should pick up some more meat? We don't want to be faced with a food shortage out in the wilderness. If you're not doing anything later, let's head over to the supermarket together.... Call me up when you get home from work.

Regards,

Martin

我正在想咱们野营准备的食物够不够。也许咱们该再多带点儿肉类食品？大家肯定不愿意在野外忍饥挨饿。如果你一会儿没什么事的话，咱们一起去超市吧……下班到家后给我打电话。

信例 2（商务类）

Dear Howard,

I think we now have enough material to start writing next month's cover story on robotics. I'm sending you a few attachments to look over, including a transcript of my phone interview with that roboticist at Tsinghua University. If you're free this afternoon, perhaps we can get started on the first draft.

Best regards,

Marsha

我觉得咱们手里的资料已经足够充分，可以开始写下个月关于机器人的那期封面故事了。我刚刚给你发了几封邮件，附件里有我电话采访一位清华大学机器人学家的访谈实录。如果你今天下午有空，咱们可以开始写初稿了。

63 过量 Excess

❶ I made a cake today, but I added too much sugar.

今天我做了一个蛋糕，不过糖放得太多了。

❷ I heard that Vicky got another speeding ticket yesterday.

我听说维姬昨天因为超速又被开了罚单。

❸ He gambled all of his earnings away and ended up penniless.

他输光了所有的钱，变得身无分文。

❹ She was disqualified from the speech competition for exceeding the time limit.

她因为超时而被取消了演讲比赛的参赛资格。

❺ The hiring manager told me that I was overqualified for the position.

聘用经理认为我在这里工作是大材小用。

❻ My family doctor told me that I have high blood pressure.

我的家庭医生告诉我，我的血压有点儿高。

❼ The new pants I bought yesterday are a bit too long.

我昨天买的新裤子有点儿太长了。

❽ The physician told Tara that she was overweight.

那个医生告诉塔拉，她超重了。

信例1（生活类）

Hi Jessie,

I went to sleep late last night and overslept this morning, so I ended up being 20 minutes late for today's midterm! Could you do me a favor? I have another exam tomorrow morning at 8:00. Since you usually get up early, could you call me around 7:30 to make sure I'm up? Thanks a million!

Yours,

Mandy

我昨晚睡得太晚结果今天早上睡过头了，导致今天的期中考试迟到了 20 分钟！你能帮我个忙吗？我明天上午 8 点钟还有另一个考试。你平时都起得很早，可不可以在 7:30 的时候给我打个电话，叫我起床呢？万分感谢！

信例2（商务类）

Dear Arthur,

My physician confirmed my suspicions yesterday and told me that I'm overweight. I exercise regularly, but I've definitely been neglecting my diet. Do you think it's too late to change my eating habits? Maybe I should follow your lead and pack a lunch to work, instead of eating fast food all the time.

Best regards,

Gwyneth

医生昨天证实了我的猜测，说我超重了。我一直都坚持锻炼的，不过肯定没有注意饮食。你觉得我从现在开始改变饮食习惯会不会太迟了？也许我该向你学习，每天中午自己带饭，而不要总吃快餐。

第十部分　说明性质
Describing Properties

64 形状 Shape/Form

❶ I bought a pair of bell-bottoms yesterday. ／ 我昨天买了一条上窄下宽的喇叭裤。

❷ Do you know where I can buy a circular coffee table? ／ 你知不知道哪里可以买到圆形的咖啡桌?

❸ The city I grew up in was laid out in a grid pattern. ／ 我从小在这座到处都有网格图案的城市里长大。

❹ Warren said his new girlfriend has long and wavy hair. ／ 华伦说他的新女友留着一头长卷发。

❺ I took lots of photos of the arched bridges in St. Petersburg. ／ 我在圣匹兹堡拍了许多拱桥的照片。

❻ My teacher described Italy's mainland as having the shape of a boot. ／ 我的老师形容意大利大陆的形状像一只靴子。

❼ He bought her a pair of heart-shaped earrings for their anniversary. ／ 他为她买了一对心形耳环作为结婚周年纪念的礼物。

❽ She has a round face and a flat nose. ／ 她的脸圆圆的，鼻子扁扁的。

信例1（生活类）

Hi Lucy,

Now that spring is here again, I've made up my mind to set up a flower bed in my front yard. I've already installed a circular-shaped frame, but I still don't know what kinds of flowers to plant. You have a lot of gardening experience.... Do you have any suggestions for me?

Yours,

Cecelia

春天又到了，我打算在我家前院整理出一个花圃来。现在已经搭好了一个圆形的架子，可是我还没想好要种些什么花。你在园艺方面经验很丰富……可不可以给我提些建议呢?

信例 2（商务类）

Dear Jacob,

I had a chance to look at your design for the new software's user interface. You've done a superb job in every respect. The only suggestion I'd like to make is to modify the shape of the buttons from elliptical to rectangular. I think that would create a sharper, more professional look.

Thanks,

Marcus

我看过了你设计的新软件的用户界面。你做得太棒了，简直是天衣无缝！我唯一的建议是按钮的形状可以做一些调整，把椭圆的改成长方形的。这样看起来更有锐气、更专业。

65　颜色 Color

1. His skin was all red after he got sunburned last weekend.
   上周末被晒伤之后，他的皮肤都变红了。

2. Her natural hair color is brown, but she likes to dye it blonde.
   她的头发天生是棕色的，不过她喜欢染成金色。

3. I really like the color of your new jacket.
   我很喜欢你新夹克的颜色。

4. Everything in my bedroom is blue, except for my furniture.
   除了家具，我卧室里其余的东西都是蓝色的。

5. Red is said to be the most visually-arresting color.
   红色据说是最具视觉冲击力的颜色。

6. Do you know how many colors there are in the rainbow?
   你知道彩虹有多少种颜色吗？

信例 1（生活类）

Hi Lara,

It's a pity that you couldn't come with us to the fireworks show last night. It was amazing to see the nighttime sky light up with all the colors of the rainbow. I'm sending you some pictures to give you an idea of what you missed. I hope we can all go together next time!

Yours,

Millie

昨晚你没来跟我们一起看焰火表演真是太遗憾了。夜晚的天空被彩虹般的七彩焰火点亮，那景色真是美不胜收。我给你发了几张照片，你看看就会知道自己错过了什么。希望下次我们能一起赏烟花。

信例 2（商务类）

Dear Elena,

I've been rethinking the color scheme we discussed for the new product package. It might be better to avoid pastel colors. Instead, let's try using a deep brown for the background, and a combination of red, green and white for the foreground text and images. See if you can finish a sketch by tomorrow.

Thanks,

Benjamin

我重新考虑了上次我们讨论过的新产品套装的颜色。我觉得还是尽量不要用浅色比较好。我们可以试试用深棕色做底色，前景的文字和图案用红、绿和白色。如果明天你能把草图做出来，咱们再讨论。

66 材料 Material

❶ I want to buy some mahogany furniture. 我想买一些红木家具。

❷ I prefer feather pillows to cotton or foam ones. 比起棉质或是海绵枕头，我更喜欢羽绒枕。

❸ I bought all the ingredients needed to make a cherry pie. 我买了制作樱桃派所需要的所有原料。

❹ The greeting cards I bought are made from 80% recycled paper. 我买的贺卡是用80%的再生纸做的。

❺ Please make sure to print the letters on 25% cotton paper. 请用含25%棉质的纸打印这封信。

❻ Zelda is regarded as an expert in plastic explosives. 萨尔达是可塑炸药方面的专家。

❼ Alice has a large collection of porcelain teacups. 爱丽丝收藏了大量的陶瓷茶具。

❽ Their new house was constructed primarily of glass and steel. 他们的新房子主要是用玻璃和钢材建造的。

❾ He bought his fiancée a pair of pearl earrings. 他给他的未婚妻买了一对珍珠耳环。

❿ She likes to wear 100% cotton T-shirts. 她喜欢穿100%纯棉T恤。

Hey Rosa,

How was your day? I bought a pair of leather shoes this afternoon … the heel is 2.5 inches, but they have foam insoles and are really comfortable! I might return those suede shoes I bought last Sunday … I don't really care for the color. By the way, do you have any plans for this weekend yet?

Love,

Bonnie

你最近过得怎么样？我今天下午买了一双皮鞋，鞋跟有 2.5 英寸高。不过里面有一层海绵的垫衬，穿起来舒服极了！也许我该把上周日买的那双仿麂皮鞋退掉……我实在是不喜欢那个颜色。顺便问一句，这个周末你有什么安排吗？

Dear Teresa,

The customer whom we held talks with yesterday called to modify his initial request. His new specifications for the T-shirts are 90% cotton and 10% polyester, rather than 100% cotton. Please provide me with a revised cost estimate ASAP so that I can fax him a new quote.

Thanks,

Brandon Hill

昨天上午跟我们通过话的那位客户刚刚打电话来要修改订单要求。他要把原定的 100% 纯棉衬衫改成成分为 90% 棉、10% 涤纶的。请你尽快给我估算一个新的成本，我好把新报价单传真给他。

67 感觉 Feeling

❶ I have a burning sensation in my chest.　　我心中热血沸腾。

❷ I felt really excited the first time I got on an airplane.　　我第一次上飞机的时候非常兴奋。

❸ I have a strong feeling that my luck is going to get better.　　我有强烈的预感我的运气会变好。

❹ I lost all feeling in my mouth after the dentist anesthetized me.　　牙医给我打了麻药之后我整个口腔都没有知觉了。

❺ I thought I heard someone entering the house last night, but it was probably just the wind.

昨晚我觉得我听到有人进入了房间，不过很可能只是风。

❻ Bill was overjoyed when he found out that he got the scholarship.

比尔获得奖学金之后狂喜不已。

❼ Conrad has learned to rely on his other senses since developing blindness.

康拉德目盲以后学会了如何靠其他感官生活。

❽ We are deeply saddened to hear about this terrible tragedy.

听到这个惨剧我们都非常悲痛。

❾ It feels awkward when she stares at me all the time.

她一直盯着我看，使我感到很不自在。

❿ He has no sense of time at all.

他毫无时间观念。

⓫ She has an excellent sense of direction.

她的方向感非常好。

信例 1（生活类）

Hi Heidi,

I'm sorry that you've been feeling down recently. Whenever I get the blues, I simply take a day off and go for massage therapy. It can relax your muscles as well as your mind. Do you want to go to the massage parlor together this weekend? Call me when you get home and let me know.

Yours,

Maureen

听说你最近心情不好，我很难过。每当我情绪低落的时候，我就会请一天假然后去做按摩治疗。它既有助于放松肌肉也可以帮你放松心情。这个周末你愿意跟我一起去按摩院吗？到家之后打电话告诉我。

信例 2（商务类）

Dear Ellen,

I've been in contact all week with the purchasing manager of Apex Clothiers, Inc. Through my conversations with her, I have a good feeling about the prospects of next week's contract negotiations. She's scheduled to fly into Chongqing next Friday and will be staying for three days. Would you mind making her hotel reservations?

Sincerely,

Gao Cheng

我跟顶峰服饰公司的采购部经理接洽了整整一个星期。通过和她的谈话，我觉得下周和他们公司关于合同的协商谈判会很成功。她下周五要飞往重庆，在那里停留 3 天。你可以帮我给她预订一下旅馆的房间吗？

68　质地 Texture

❶ I love the texture of the scarf you gave me. 　　我喜欢你送我的那条围巾的质地。

❷ I prefer matte-finish photographs to glossy ones. 　　比起光面照片我更喜欢亚光的。

❸ I can't stand the mushy texture of overcooked noodles. 　　煮过头的粘糊糊的面条让我难以忍受。

❹ The vinyl jacket I bought feels just like leather. 　　我买的那件聚乙烯基夹克摸起来像是皮质的。

❺ Dora prides herself on her silky smooth hair. 　　多拉为自己拥有一头丝般顺滑的头发而自豪。

❻ It's hard to tell whether a peach is ripe based solely on its texture. 　　单从肉质上很难分辨出桃子是否熟了。

❼ Soft sweatpants are a lot more comfy than stiff denim jeans. 　　柔软的针织运动裤比硬布牛仔裤穿起来舒服多了。

❽ My skin gets dry and rough every winter. 　　我的皮肤每到冬天就会变得干燥粗糙。

信例 1（生活类）

Hi Becky,

How was your weekend? I just wanted to thank you again for the beautiful cashmere sweater.... I'm wearing it today, and I just love its soft, smooth texture! All of my other sweaters are made of ordinary wool or synthetic fibers, so I never realized how lightweight and comfortable cashmere is. Thanks again!

Warmest regards,

Felicia

周末过得如何？我就是想再次感谢你送我那件漂亮的羊绒衫……我今天穿上了，真喜欢它那种柔软、顺滑的质地。我以前所有的毛衣都是普通羊毛或合成纤维的，所以我从来不知道羊绒衫会这么轻、这么舒服。再次感谢！

信例 2（商务类）

Dear Ms. Bell,

I'm attaching a high-resolution image of our revised corporate brochure. We would like to have 2,500 copies printed. As usual, please use the 70-pound bond paper with matte finish. There isn't any hurry, so just let me know when the brochures are ready and I'll arrange someone to pick them up.

Sincerely yours,

Simon Hayes

通过附件发给您一份我公司新的宣传册，该图片是高分辨率的。我们想印 2500 张。请用和以往一样的 70 磅亚光文件纸。这一批不是很急，印好之后您通知我，我派人去取就行。

69 价值 Value

❶ I bought a new bicycle in China for 500 RMB.

我在中国花了 500 元人民币买了一辆新的自行车。

❷ His income last year totaled approximately $80,000.

他去年的总收入接近 8 万美元。

❸ Her company suffered a net loss of 12 million euro last year.

她的公司去年净亏损 1200 万欧元。

❹ Does your hotel have a safe where guests can store their valuables?

贵酒店有能保存客人贵重物品的地方吗?

❺ Eric told me that he's unwilling to sell his land at any price.

埃里克告诉我无论对方出什么价钱他都不愿意卖掉他的地。

❻ In some countries, sales tax is included in marked prices.

有些国家商品的售价里是包含销售税金的。

❼ I'm sure your trip will be a very worthwhile experience.

我保证您会不虚此行。

❽ I recommend that you have your antiques appraised.

我建议您应该给您的古董作一个估价。

❾ The new grocery store has very reasonable prices.

新开的杂货店价格非常公道。

❿ Your suggestions are extremely valuable to me.

您的建议对我非常宝贵。

⓫ Thank you for the precious gifts you sent us.

谢谢你送给我们的珍贵礼物。

信例1（生活类）

Hi Mitch,

After our conversation last week, I decided to have my house reappraised. Much to my surprise, the estimated market value is up 60% from the last appraisal five years ago! Still, I'm not sure whether I should sell it now ... or wait for it to further appreciate. What would you advise?

Regards,

Stephanie

我们上周谈过之后，我决定对我的房子进行重新估价。让我大吃一惊的是，对房价的估测比5年前上涨了六成。我正在犹豫是否要在这个时候卖掉房子，或者再等一等也许以后价格会更高。你觉得呢？

信例2（商务类）

Dear Ms. Taylor,

Based on the findings of our market research, the retail value of the new software should be somewhere between ＄600 and ＄625. Given current markups, it should be feasible to set a manufacturer's price of at least ＄500. I've attached the market research report and price calculations for your review.

Sincerely,

Norman Roberts

根据我们最近的市场调查显示，新软件的零售价格应该定在600美元至625美元之间。鉴于目前的涨价幅度，我们应该把出厂价至少定为500美元才比较合理。我已经把市场调查报告和估价单都放在附件里了，请您过目。

第十一部分　说明数值
Describing Numerical Values

70 基础运算 Basic arithmetic

❶ Momentum equals mass multiplied by velocity.   动量等于质量与速度的乘积。

❷ Current is equal to voltage divided by resistance.   电流等于电压除以电阻。

❸ Profit equals income minus expenditure.   利润等于收入减去成本。

❹ The sum of the angles of any triangle is 180 degrees.   三角形的内角之和是 180 度。

❺ I noticed that my bill was added incorrectly.   我发现我的账单被算错了。

❻ Frank can multiply large numbers in his head.   弗兰克可以心算大数的乘积。

信例 1（生活类）

Hi Tiffany,

Just got back from the mall … you'll never guess the deal I got. Remember that skirt we saw at Genoa Outlet last week? It was 70% off! The original price was $500, but I only paid like 150 bucks! The sale is on all week … wanna go shopping together again on Friday?

Yours,

Christina

还是接着说在商场购物的事吧……你肯定想不到我赶上了什么好事。记得上周咱们在热那亚上品折扣店看到的那条裙子吗？现在居然 3 折啦！原价 500 美元，而我只花了 150 块！这次打折活动要持续整整一周……想不想周五再跟我去逛逛？

信例 2（商务类）

Dear Evelyn,
I checked the ticket prices for all flights from Jakarta to Manila leaving on April 20. The lowest prices are for a seven-hour flight departing at 1:35 pm; business class seats are available for $761.25 ($725.00 plus 5% tax). If you would like to book a ticket, please let me know as soon as possible.
Best regards,
Sonya Reed

我查了 4 月 20 日从雅加达飞往马尼拉的所有航班价格。票价最低的是下午 1:35 起飞，全程 7 小时，商务舱，761.25 美元（725 美元再加 5% 的税金），如果你想订一张票，请尽快通知我。

71 倍数和百分比 Multiples and percentages

❶ The price of oil has doubled in less than two years.

不到两年，石油的价格翻了一番。

❷ The new school library will be twice as large as the old one.

新的学校图书馆是原来的两倍大。

❸ His fortune has more than tripled in the past six months.

在过去的 6 个月里，他的财富暴增至原来的 3 倍。

❹ Her new house is about five times bigger than her old one.

她的新房子比旧房子大 5 倍。

❺ I got 85% on my English essay and 75% on my math quiz.

我的英语论文得了 85 分，数学测验得了 75 分。

❻ He decided to invest 30 percent of his savings in the stock market.

他决定把自己存款的 30% 投资到股市中。

❼ She spends over 50 percent of her time conducting research.

她花了多一半的时间用来进行研究。

❽ Our company's earnings rose by 10% this quarter.

这个季度我们公司的盈利上升了 10%。

Hi Brett,

Do you know what the interest rate on your savings account is? I asked at my bank yesterday, and they said it's only around 1.5%. The inflation rate last year was over 2% ... so in reality I'm probably losing money. Do you think I'd be better off putting my money in mutual funds or something?

Best regards,

Amelia

你知道你的存款利率是多少吗？我昨天去银行问了，他们告诉我只有 1.5% 左右。而去年的通货膨胀率超过了 2% 呢……所以实际上我几乎等于在赔钱。你觉得我是不是该把钱取出来投资到共同基金或是其他什么方面去？

Dear Tom,

Frankly, I wasn't surprised to learn that our European market share has dropped 2% over the past year. What does surprise me is our growing market share in Asia—3% to 8% over the past 12 months. We need to look for ways to reverse the downward trend in Europe while maintaining our growth in Asia.

Regards,

Lawrence

坦白地说，去年一年我们在欧洲的市场占有率下降了将近2%，我并不为此感到惊讶。但是去年我们在亚洲的市场占有率从3%上升到了8%，这倒让我大吃一惊。我们接下来需要做的是寻求一种解决办法，在保证亚洲市场增长的同时扭转欧洲市场不景气的现状。

72 增加和减少 Increase and decrease

❶ I've been spending more and more time on the phone lately.

我最近打电话的时间越来越多了。

❷ If we don't increase our production capacity, we may begin to lose clients.

如果我们不提高生产能力，就会失去很多客户。

❸ The shares I bought last week have fallen slightly in value.

上周我买的股票跌了一点儿。

④ My family is looking for ways to cut down on waste.　　　我家正在想办法节约开支。

⑤ After switching jobs, his monthly salary jumped from 20,000 RMB to 30,000 RMB.　　　换工作后，他的月收入从 2 万涨到3 万人民币。

⑥ In the last three months, her weight dropped from 150 pounds to under 125 pounds.　　　在过去的 3 个月里，她的体重从150 磅降到125 磅以下。

⑦ Since starting my diet last year, my waist size has shrunk three inches.　　　自从我去年开始节食以来，我的腰围已经缩小 3 英寸了。

⑧ My doctor recommended that I eat more fruits and vegetables.　　　我的医生建议我再多吃些蔬菜和水果。

⑨ We've greatly improved efficiency at the factory this year.　　　今年我们工厂的工作效率得到了大幅度提高。

信例1（生活类）

Hey Sam,

Did you hear that the unemployment rate has dropped to below 2 percent? That ought to improve our chances of finding summer jobs this year. I still remember last summer, when even volunteering positions were hard to come by! Anyways, since it's already April, we should probably start our job search soon.

See you at school,

Darlene

你听说了吗？失业率已经下降到 2% 以下了。这就意味着咱们今年夏天找到工作的机会大大增加。我还记得去年夏天，即便是做义工的工作都很难找到。不管怎么说，现在已经是 4 月份了，咱们该尽快动手找工作了。

Dear Hugh,

One of our major clients called and asked whether their monthly order could be increased from 75,000 to 100,000 units. I'm aware that current production is at full capacity. Are there any bottlenecks in the production line? I want you to see if we can increase our maximum capacity and how much it would cost.

Thanks,

Russell

我们的一个主要客户刚刚打电话过来，询问他们每月订购的数量是否可以从 7.5 万件增加到 10 万件。我知道咱们目前的产量已经满负荷了。生产线方面有什么障碍吗？我希望你能调查一下，看看咱们是否能把最高产量再提升一些，另外，这部分所需要的成本是多少。

73 基础测量（长、宽等）

Basic measurements（length, width, etc.）

❶ The tallest student in my class is 190 centimeters tall.　　我们班最高的学生有 190 厘米高。

❷ My garden is about 30 feet long and 20 feet wide.　　我的花园长约 30 英尺，宽约 20 英尺。

❸ The island has a perimeter of 40 kilometers.　　这个岛的周长是 40 公里。

❹ The Great Wall of China spans a length of 7,300 kilometers.　　中国的长城绵延 7300 公里。

❺ Jade Dragon Snow Mountain has an elevation of 5,596 meters.　　玉龙雪山有 5596 米高。

❻ The deepest point of the lake is about 250 meters deep.　　这个湖最深的地方约有 250 米深。

❼ His new laptop computer is only 0.75 inches thick.　　他的新笔记本电脑厚度仅为 0.75 英寸。

❽ Her hair was over two feet long when she had it cut.　　剪发之前，她的头发足有 2 英尺多长。

信例1（生活类）

Hi Alyssa,

We just had a swimming pool installed in our backyard over the weekend. It's not that big—30 feet long, 12 feet wide, and 5 feet deep—but it's good enough for taking a dip. Would you be interested in coming over tomorrow after work for a swim? Call me and let me know. :)

Yours,

Joanna

我们利用上个周末在我家后院里安了一个游泳池。不算太大——30 英尺长、12 英尺宽、5 英尺深——但足够让人游会儿泳的。你有兴趣明天下班之后来游个泳吗？如果想的话打个电话告诉我。

信例2（商务类）

Hi Duane,

Are you interested in an almost-new computer desk? I'm moving on Sunday to a place that's already furnished ... and I'd rather give the desk to someone than sell it secondhand. The dimensions are 80 cm（height）x 150 cm（width）x 60 cm（depth）. Just let me know at work tomorrow if you want it.

Best regards,

Gregory

你想不想要一个九成新的电脑桌？这个周日我要搬家，新家里家具都齐全了……我不想把这个电脑桌当作二手货卖掉，而是想送给朋友。这个桌子的尺寸是 80 厘米（长）× 150 厘米（宽）× 60 厘米（高）。如果你想要的话，请明天上班的时候告诉我。

74 近似值和平均值 Approximate value and average value

近似值 Approximate value

❶ Over 250 people have signed up for the conference.

本次会议共有 250 多人报名参加。

❷ There are about 500 students in my psychology class.

我的心理学课约有 500 个学生。

❸ The city has a history spanning almost 1,000 years.

这个城市几乎有 1000 年的历史。

④ Gary said he has a grade point average of about 3.95.　　加里说他的平均分大概是 3.95。

⑤ I spend about two hours every day writing e-mails.　　我每天要花 2 小时左右写电子邮件。

⑥ I paid around 200 RMB for my last haircut.　　我上次剪头发花了大约 200 块钱。

⑦ The temperature fell to around five degrees yesterday.　　昨天的气温下降到 5 度左右。

⑧ The author's latest book is roughly 300 pages long.　　这个作家最新的作品大约有 300 页。

平均值 *Average value*

① The average lifespan has risen in the past 25 years.　　在过去的 25 年间，平均寿命有所增加。

② The average annual temperature here is 20 degrees Celsius.　　这里的年平均气温是 20 摄氏度。

③ The average precipitation in April is 64 millimeters.　　4 月份的平均降水量是 64 毫米。

④ I get an average of eight hours of sleep per night.　　我平均每天的睡眠是 8 个小时。

⑤ I watch five movies a month on average.　　我平均每月看 5 部电影。

⑥ The river has an average depth of two feet.　　这条河的平均深度为 2 英尺。

⑦ On average, Helen writes two screenplays a year.　　海伦平均每年写两个电影剧本。

信例 1（生活类）

Hi Sue,

I heard that there's a new exhibition on China at the World Civilizations Museum starting next week. It's supposed to include over 3,000 objects spanning around 5,000 years of Chinese history. Would you be interested in going? The museum is open late on Fridays … maybe we could go on Friday evening after work.

Best regards,

Bernie

我听说下周在世界文明博物馆要举办一个关于中国的新展览。届时将展出中国上下五千年历史中的 3000 件文物。你想去看一看吗？这家博物馆周五闭馆比较晚……或许咱们可以星期五下班之后过去看看。

信例2（商务类）

Dear Mr. Allen,

As per your request, please find attached a copy of last month's sales report. Average daily sales were ＄8,125, compared with ＄7,975 last month and ＄6,325 for the same period last year. I'm currently preparing next month's sales forecast and will send it to you by this afternoon.

Sincerely yours,

Zachary Carter

我已经把您要的上个月的销售报告放在附件里了。报告显示我们的日销售额达到了8125美元，与上个月的7975美元和去年同期的6325美元相比都有提高。我正在写下个月的销售预测，今天下午写好之后发送给您。

75 比率和比例 Ratios and proportions

❶ The teacher-student ratio at my son's new school is 1:15.

我儿子新学校的师生比为1:15。

❷ My city has a population density of over 3,000 people per square kilometer.

我市的人口密度是每平方公里3000多人。

❸ Blood pressure can be expressed as the ratio of systolic pressure over diastolic pressure.

血压可表示为收缩压与舒张压的比值。

❹ I think the garden is disproportionately large for such a small house.

对这所小房子而言，我认为它的花园大得不成比例。

❺ A large proportion of my colleagues were sick last month.

上个月我的大部分同事都生病了。

❻ What proportion of your income do you spend on food?

你在食品上的花费占收入的比例是多少？

Hi Burt,

As you know, my daughter is in her last year of junior high school. I'm worried that the large class sizes are affecting her education, so I'd like her to attend a high school with a lower student-teacher ratio. Could I ask you which private school your son is attending? How are the class sizes?

Best regards,

Cheryl

我女儿今年已经是初中三年级了。她们班的学生人数太多，我怕对她的学习有不好的影响，所以想给她找一所学生和教师人数比例低一点的高中——20:1 比较合适，当然再低一些更好。你儿子上的是哪所私立学校？大概一个班有多少学生呢？

Dear Mr. Berg,

I've finished tabulating the customer transaction data you requested. Last month, approximately two-thirds of all transactions were made through our website—an increase of one-third from a year ago. Moreover, online purchases accounted for some four-fifths of last month's sales revenues. A summary and analysis of the data is attached for your review.

Regards,

Kevin Brooks

我已经按照您的要求把客户交易数据的表格做好了。上个月我们网站的交易额接近总交易额的 2/3，比去年增长了 1/3。而且，上个月的在线购物营业额已达到总销售额的 4/5。相关的数据总结和分析报告请见附件。

76 最大值和最小值 Maximums and minimums

❶ The teacher said the essay should be at least 5,000 words long.

老师说这篇论文至少要写 5000 字。

❷ I heard that the new train has a top speed of 350 miles per hour.

我听说新型火车的最快时速是 350 英里。

❸ I need to get a minimum of 75% on the final exam to pass the course.

期末考试我至少要考 75 分才能通过这门课。

❹ The boss gave us a maximum of 10 days to finish this project.

我的上司让我们最多用 10 天来完成这个项目。

信例1（生活类）

Hey Liz,

If you rent a car on your trip to the States, just remember that some roads have minimum speeds in addition to speed limits. Some of the interstate highways, for example, have posted minimum speeds of 40 mph. I know that you're a cautious driver ... but just make sure not to drive too slowly!

Best wishes,

Bradley

如果你去美国旅游想租车上路，一定要记住：有些公路除了有最高限速之外，还有最低限速。比如，一些州际高速公路上都有最低限速 40 英里/小时的限速牌。我知道你开车很谨慎……不过千万别开得太慢了！

信例2（商务类）

Dear Mr. Price,

Thank you for your inquiry. Due to limited availability, the maximum order quantity for our handmade porcelain dolls is currently restricted to 10 per customer. However, no quantity restrictions apply to our other products, including plastic dolls, building blocks, and model cars. Please let us know if you have any additional questions.

Sincerely,

Dwight Nelson

感谢您的质询。由于制作能力有限，我们手工制作的陶瓷娃娃每位客户最多只能购买 10 个。不过，我们的其他产品包括：塑料娃娃、积木和汽车模型都是敞开供应的，没有数量限制。如果您还有其他问题，欢迎垂询。

第十二部分 通知
Making Notices

77 通知开会 Announcing meetings

❶ The next staff meeting will be held on Monday, January 10 at 10:00 am.

下一次员工大会将于 1 月 10 日(周一)上午 10 点召开。

❷ Refreshments will be provided/served at the meeting.

会上供应茶点。

❸ Attendance is mandatory for all members.

所有成员都必须出席本会。

❹ Please see the attachment for a complete list of upcoming meetings.

近期会议一览表请见附件。

❺ Please refer to the attached meeting agenda for details.

具体情况请参见附件里的会议日程。

信例1

Dear Members,
Please note that a meeting of the fundraising committee will be held on Monday, September 15 at 2:30 pm in Alexander Hall, Room 201. Attendance is required only for fundraising committee members, but all members are encouraged to attend. Please visit our club's website for a full list of upcoming meetings and events.
Sincerely yours,
Leon Jenkins

请注意,筹款委员会将于 9 月 15 日(周一)下午 2:30 在亚历山大大楼 201 室召开会议。出席者只限于筹款委员会成员,不过欢迎其他员工列席旁听。近期的会议和活动通知请登陆我们的会员网站。

信例 2

Dear Managers,

This is to inform you that the next planning meeting will be held on Wednesday, March 25 at 2:00 pm in Room 301. All junior and senior managers are expected to attend. Please review the attached meeting agenda as soon as possible, and contact me if there is anything you wish to have added.

Sincerely,

Loyd Miller

在此通知各位下一次会议将于 3 月 25 日（周三）下午两点在 301 室召开。请初级和中级的所有负责人届时出席。请各位尽快浏览附件里的会议日程，如果有需要添加的内容请与我联系。

78 更改开会时间 Changing the meeting time

❶ Please note that the next staff meeting has been rescheduled.

请注意下次员工会议已变更日期。

❷ The meeting will now be held on Wednesday, February 25 at 2:00 pm.

会议现改为 2 月 25 日（周三）下午两点召开。

❸ Please note that the March 12 fundraising meeting has been moved to March 15.

请注意筹款会议的召开日期由 3 月 12 日改为 3 月 15 日。

❹ Due to a scheduling conflict, tomorrow's meeting has been postponed until next week.

由于时间冲突，定于明天召开的会议延至下周。

❺ The new date and time will be announced tomorrow.

更改后的会议时间将于明日另行通知。

❻ We apologize for the inconvenience.

为此所带来的不便请您谅解。

Dear Staff Members,
Please note that the upcoming school board meeting—previously scheduled for Monday, November 1—has been moved to Friday, November 5 from 9:30 to 11:30 am. As usual, the meeting will be held in the conference room of the Central Administration Building. We look forward to seeing you all there.
Regards,
Kathleen Jackson

请注意即将召开的教育委员会会议——原定于 11 月 1 日（周一）——现改为 11 月 5 日（周五）上午 9:30 到 11:30。同往常一样，会议将在中央行政楼的会议室召开。希望届时能见到大家。

Dear Colleagues,
Please be advised that, due to office renovations, tomorrow morning's meeting has been rescheduled to Tuesday, June 20. The time and room will be announced by the end of the day. Thank you for your attention to this matter and I apologize for any inconvenience.
Sincerely,
Wallace Sanders

由于办公室装修，原定于明天上午的会议改至 6 月 20 日（周二）召开。会议的具体时间和地点将会在下班前另行通知。谢谢大家的关注，对因此带来的任何不便我深表歉意。

79 通知做预算 Requesting budgets

❶ Please prepare a preliminary budget for the next fiscal year. 请为下一个财政年度做一个初步预算。

❷ The budget should be submitted electronically on or before April 12. 预算报告请于 4 月 12 日前以电子版形式提交。

❸ This is a reminder that first-quarter budgets should be submitted by tomorrow. 提醒各位第一季度的预算报告请于明日提交。

❹ If you have any questions or concerns, please feel free to contact me. 如有任何问题请与我联系。

⑤ Please refer to the attached budget template and guidelines. 请参见附件里的预算模板和标准。

信例 1

Dear Department Heads,
This is a reminder that third-quarter budgets for each department should be submitted on or before September 18. Please use the provided template, and submit the completed budget in both hard- and soft-copy formats. If you anticipate any difficulty in meeting this deadline, please contact me as soon as possible.
Sincerely,
Eleanor Patterson

请于 9 月 18 日之前把各部门第三季度的预算报告递交我处。请按照我们先前提供的模板填写，并将内容复制软盘、硬盘各一份上交。如有任何困难不能在上述日期之前提交预算，请尽快与我联系。

信例 2

Dear Store Managers,
As the year-end is approaching, we would like to ask each store manager to prepare a preliminary budget for the coming fiscal year. A sample budget is attached for your reference. If you have any questions, please feel free to contact me at your convenience. Your cooperation is greatly appreciated.
Sincerely,
Nathan Campbell

岁末将至，我们想请每个商店经理为下一个财政年度做一份初步预算。附件里有一份预算模板，仅供参考。如有任何问题请在方便的时候随时与我联系。谢谢您的合作。

80 申请购买办公用品 Applying to purchase office articles

❶ I would like to request the purchase of a new photocopier for our department. 我想为本部门申请购买一台新复印机。

❷ The current photocopier has already broken down three times this month. 现在使用的复印机本月已经坏过 3 次了。

❸ A new photocopier would improve efficiency and, ultimately, reduce costs. 新购置一台复印机可以提高效率，最终降低成本。

❹ Thank you in advance for your 提前感谢您的关心。
consideration.

信例 1

Dear Ms. Wright,
In order to facilitate our sales team in delivering presentations to current and prospective clients, I would like to apply for the purchase of a digital projector. The attached application details the projector's intended use and lists product information, including model, price and technical specifications. Thank you very much for your consideration.
Yours sincerely,
Donald Perry

为便于我们销售人员向客户（包括现有客户与潜在客户）更好地讲解并演示产品，特向您申请购买一部数码投影仪。附件里有一份申请书，上面已经写明投影仪的具体用途和产品的具体信息，包括：型号、价格和技术参数。感谢您的关注。

信例 2

Dear Mr. Guo,
I would like to request the purchase of a new laser printer for the accounting department. The current printer has had frequent mechanical problems, resulting in high repair costs; it is no longer covered by warranty. A new printer would improve efficiency and, ultimately, reduce expenses. Your consideration is very much appreciated.
Sincerely,
Meng Zheng

我想为财务部申请购买一台新的激光打印机。现有的这台频繁出现机械故障，因此维修费用较高，而且也已经不在保修期内了。购买一台新打印机可以提高工作效率，也能最终降低费用。感谢您对这个问题能予以考虑。

81 通知放假 Announcing holidays

❶ We are pleased to announce that, beginning next year, all full-time employees will be given two additional vacation days.

我们很高兴地向大家宣布，从明年起所有全职员工都将享受到多加的两天假期。

❷ If you have any questions, please contact me at your convenience.

如有问题请在方便的时候与我联系。

信例 1

Dear Colleagues,
We are pleased to announce that, beginning next year, the base number of vacation days for all employees will be increased from 10 to 12 days. The total number of vacation days will still be determined by each employee's length of service. If you have any questions, please do not hesitate to contact me.
Sincerely,
Jared Coleman

我们非常高兴地通知大家一个好消息：从明年起，所有员工的基本假期都将从 10 天增加至 12 天。休假总天数最终将按照每位员工的工作年限而定。如有什么问题，请尽管与我联系。

信例 2

Dear Colleagues,
To express our appreciation for your hard work this year and enable everyone to spend the holidays with friends and family, we've decided to close the office from December 25 to January 1, inclusive. All personnel will be given paid leave during this period. We wish you all a happy and healthy holiday season.
Sincerely,
Douglas Brown

为了表示对各位一年来辛勤工作的感谢，同时也为了能让各位能和家人朋友一起尽情享受假期，我们决定从 12 月 25 日当天开始放假直至 1 月 1 日。这段时间里，所有员工都将享受带薪休假。祝愿大家有一个快乐健康的假期。

82 晚会通知 Announcing parties

❶ It is with pleasure that I invite you to attend our 10th anniversary celebration.

很荣幸邀请您参加我们的结婚10周年纪念庆祝会。

❷ Our holiday party will be held on December 18th from 7:00 to 10:00 pm at East Redwood Hotel.

我们的节日酒会将于12月18日晚7点至10点在东红杉酒店举办。

❸ Dinner and refreshments will be provided.

晚会提供晚宴及茶点。

❹ Please feel free to bring your family and friends.

请携家人及朋友出席。

信例 1

Dear Colleagues,

It is with great pleasure that I invite you to attend our 20th anniversary celebration on June 15. We will be meeting at 6:00 pm at Dimensions Bar and Grill for dinner, after which we will proceed to the nearby Triple Axis Lounge for drinks and dancing. Please invite your friends and family to join us.

Sincerely,

Wesley Green

我很荣幸地邀请各位于6月15日出席我和夫人的结婚20周年纪念庆祝晚宴。宴会将于晚上6:00在维度烧烤餐厅举办，晚餐结束后我们将会移至附近的三轴休闲吧喝酒跳舞。请邀请朋友和家人一起参加。

信例 2

Dear Colleagues,

We are pleased to announce that our holiday office party will be held at the Grand Oasis Inn on December 20th from 6:30 to 9:30 pm. Dress is informal and refreshments will be provided. As always, you are welcome to bring along friends and family members. We look forward to seeing everyone there.

Best regards,

Sophia Williams

我们很高兴地通知大家，我们的节日宴会将于12月20日晚上6:30至9:30在绿洲大酒店举办。穿休闲服装即可，宴会时供应便餐。与以往一样，欢迎携朋友或家人出席。期待在宴会时见到各位。

83 通知人事更换 Announcing changes in leadership

❶ We are pleased to announce the appointment of Kirk Randall as our new Director of Technology, effective immediately.

很高兴向大家宣布现任命柯克·兰朵为技术总监，即时生效。

❷ With his broad knowledge and rich experience, he will certainly be an invaluable asset to our company.

他拥有丰富的知识和经验，为我公司创造的价值将无法估量。

❸ He will replace Elise Whitaker, who will be retiring at the end of this month after 25 years of dedicated service.

爱丽丝·惠特克已为我公司服务 25 年，将于本月底退休，其工作将由他接替。

信例1

Dear Faculty, Staff and Students,
It is with great pleasure that Watson University announces the appointment of Adrian Lee as Chief Financial Officer. Lee has served for 12 years as professor in the Faculty of Commerce, and brings extensive academic and business experience to his new position. He holds a Ph. D. in Law from Peking University.
Sincerely,
Brenda Adams, Chancellor

很高兴地告诉大家：沃特森大学宣布任命安德里亚·李为我校的财务主管。李教授曾在商学院任教 12 年，今后将在新的工作岗位上继续发挥他卓越的学术思想和丰富的商务经验。李教授曾就读于北京大学，并获得法学博士学位。

信例 2

Dear Colleagues,

We are pleased to announce, effective immediately, the appointment of Julia Turner as Chief Information Officer of Legend Concepts Group. Ms. Turner possesses 15 years of experience in the information technology sector and her extensive knowledge will be an invaluable asset to our company. Please join us in welcoming Ms. Turner to Legend Concepts.

Sincerely,

Marvin Barnes, President

我们很高兴地宣布，传奇概念公司的信息部总监一职将由朱莉娅·特纳担任。特纳女士在信息技术方面拥有长达 15 年的相关工作经验。她丰富的知识能为我公司带来的价值将无法估算。请大家一起为特纳女士加盟我们传奇概念公司致以热烈的欢迎。

第十三部分　访问事宜
Writing about Visiting

84 约定来访时间 Arranging the time of visit

❶ I will be in Dallas early next month on business.

我下个月初要去达拉斯出差。

❷ If possible, I would like to visit you during the first week of May.

如果条件允许，我想于 5 月的第一周到贵处参观。

❸ We are very interested in seeing your new line of packaging machines.

我们很想看看贵公司新推出的包装机械系列产品。

❹ Please let me know if this time would be convenient for you.

如果您觉得这个时间可以的话，请告诉我。

❺ I would like to visit Kansas City sometime between June 10 and 24.

我将于 6 月 10 日至 24 日期间的某日访问堪萨斯市。

❻ Could we schedule a time to meet during those two weeks?

我们可以把时间安排在那两周吗？

❼ I look forward to meeting you in Shenyang soon.

我期待尽快在沈阳与您会面。

❽ I look forward to hearing from you soon.

期待能尽快收到您的回复。

信例 1

Dear Helen,

I'm planning a trip to Qingdao from May 5 to 12. Would it be possible to visit your factory during that week? We've designed a new product and would like to bring it to market in the coming months. Please let me know your schedule. I look forward to hearing from you soon.

Best regards,

Diane Cook

我计划于 5 月 5 日至 12 日到青岛出差。那一周去您的工厂参观可以吗？我们设计出了一个新产品并打算于近期投入市场。请告诉我们您的时间安排。期待尽快收到您的回复。

Dear Ms. Turner,

In light of your schedule, I've rescheduled our visit to Denver for October 25 to 28. Could I trouble you to book accommodations for me and two of my colleagues at East Chariot Hotel for the above dates? Thank you in advance. We look forward to seeing you in Denver soon.

Yours sincerely,

Liang-Yun Shen

按照您的日程安排，我把我们去丹佛的日期调整为 10 月 25 日到 28 日。可不可以麻烦您根据上面的时间帮我和我的两个同事在东沙利奥特酒店预订一下住宿？先谢谢您了。期待能尽快在丹佛见到您。

85 欢迎来访 Welcoming the visitors

❶ I am delighted to learn that you will be visiting Wuhan next month.

知道您将于下月访问武汉的消息我很高兴。

❷ We will be glad to arrange a tour of our factory for July 3.

我们将把参观工厂的相关事宜安排在 7 月 3 日。

❸ Please let me know once you have confirmed the exact date of your arrival.

一旦您确定了到达的具体日期请通知我。

❹ Please let us know if we can arrange hotel accommodations for you.

如果需要我们为您安排酒店食宿，请通知我们。

❺ I look forward to meeting with you soon.

期待能尽快与您会面。

❻ We look forward to seeing you soon.

我们期待能很快见到您。

Dear Whitney,

I'm glad to learn that you will be visiting Toronto next month. I'll be in Montreal between February 16 and 19, so if it's convenient for you, shall we arrange to meet on the 20th? Please let me know whether I can arrange hotel accommodations and transportation from the airport for you.

Best regards,

Arnold Morris

很高兴你下个月要到多伦多来。2 月 16 日到 19 日期间我将会待在蒙特利尔，如果方便的话，咱们把见面日期定在 20 号如何？请告诉我是否需要为你安排机场的接送服务和酒店住宿。

信例2

Dear Mr. Kim,

Thank you for your reply. We would certainly be glad to arrange a tour of our factory for July 4. If you do not anticipate being too tired after your flight, may we invite you to dine with us on the evening of the 3rd? We look forward to seeing you soon.

Sincerely yours,

Huang Tao

感谢您的回复。我们很高兴地为您安排于7月4日参观我工厂。如果您7月3日那天不觉得旅途太劳顿的话，我们希望能在当晚宴请您。期待我们能尽快见面。

86 更改来访时间 Changing the time of visit

❶ Due to unforeseen circumstances, my trip has to be postponed until next month.

由于不可预知的原因，我的行程推迟至下个月。

❷ I'm very sorry for this last-minute change of plans.

我很抱歉在最后更改了计划。

❸ Please let me know whether we could possibly meet on August 18 instead of the 16th.

我们想把原定于8月16日的会面改到8月18日，不知是否可以。

❹ Because some urgent business has come up, I'll have to delay my visit until early September.

由于出现紧急公务需要处理，我得推迟访问时间至9月初。

❺ Could we arrange a meeting during the first week of October?

我们是否可以把会面安排在10月的第一周？

❻ Would it be possible to reschedule our meeting for mid-November?

可不可以把原定的会面改在11月中旬？

❼ Please let me know which day would be most convenient for you.

请告诉我您哪一天最方便。

❽ I hope this change in schedule will not cause too much inconvenience for you.

希望原定日期的变更不会给您造成太多不便。

Dear Mr. Johnson,

In our conversation last week, I said that I would be arriving in Stockholm on April 12th. Due to unforeseen circumstances, my trip will have to be postponed until the 15th. Would it be possible to reschedule our meeting? I apologize for this change and hope that it will not cause too much inconvenience.

Sincerely,

Katherine Rogers

上周我们会谈时，我说打算 4 月 12 日去斯德哥尔摩。由于一些不可预知的原因，这次行程将延迟到 15 日。可以重新安排一下我们的会面日期吗？很抱歉要更改日期，希望不会给您带来太多不便。

Dear Mr. Lai,

Unfortunately, I will be unable to arrive in Guangzhou on June 3 as anticipated. My uncle passed away yesterday, and it is important that I remain with my family at this difficult time. Would it be acceptable to reschedule the visit for mid-June? I'm very sorry for this sudden change of plans.

Regards,

Seth Mitchell

很抱歉，我原定于 6 月 3 日去广州的计划不能成行了。我叔叔昨天过世了，我觉得留下来和家人一起度过这段悲痛的时光很重要。6 月中旬再去拜访您可以吗？计划突然变更，我非常抱歉。

87 预订房间 Reservation of rooms

预订房间 *Reserving rooms*

❶ I'm planning a trip to Suzhou with two colleagues for December 5 to 8.

我计划于 12 月 5 日到 8 日和两个同事一起去苏州出差。

❷ We would greatly appreciate it if you could reserve three of your deluxe suites for us.

如果您能给我们预留三个豪华套房，我们将不胜感激。

❸ I look forward to hearing from you soon.

期待尽快收到您的回复。

答复　*Replying*

❶ Thank you for your e-mail of January 12.

谢谢您 1 月 12 日的来信。

❷ We have reserved two single rooms under your name for February 25 to March 1.

我们用您的名字预订了从 2 月 25 日到 3 月 1 日的两个单人间。

❸ As requested, we have reserved three of our premium suites for you and your colleagues.

我们已经按照您的要求为您和您的同事预订了三间高级套房。

❹ Please provide us with your credit card information so that we can hold the reservation for you.

请提供您的信用卡信息以便我们为您预订房间。

❺ We look forward to seeing you on April 5.

期待 4 月 5 日见到您。

信例 1

Dear Sir or Madam,

I'm planning a trip to New York with three colleagues for August 16-20. I understand that this is your busy season, but I would appreciate it if you could reserve either an executive suite or two double rooms for us, depending on availability. Thank you in advance. I look forward to hearing from you soon.

Sincerely,

Cynthia Phillips

我计划于 8 月 16 日至 20 日与三个同事一起去纽约。我知道这段时间恰好是旅游旺季，不过如果您能在上述时间里，为我们订一个套房或是两个双人间，我将不胜感激。先谢谢您。期待您的回复。

信例 2

Dear Ms. Zhu,

I am glad to inform you that we have booked your accommodations at Grand Galaxy Inn for March 10 to 15. As requested, we have reserved three of our deluxe suites for you and your colleagues. Please see the attached leaflet for information on your accommodations. We look forward to seeing you soon.

Yours sincerely,

Gerald Bryant

很高兴地通知您我们已经为您预订了 3 月 10 日至 15 日在格拉克斯大酒店的房间。根据您的要求，我们为您和您的同事预留了三间豪华套房。房间的详细介绍请参见附件里的宣传页。期待届时您的光临。

88 感谢热情接待

Expressing gratitude for a warm reception

❶ It was a pleasure to meet with you and your colleagues in Nashville.

很荣幸能在纳什维尔与您和您的同事见面。

❷ Thank you so much for your warm hospitality during my stay in Chengdu.

非常感谢在成都时您对我的热情款待。

❸ Please also convey my thanks to all the workers at your factory for their kindness.

请代我对贵厂工人的热情友好表示谢意。

❹ Thank you for giving us such a detailed presentation of your products.

感谢您向我们进行了如此详细的产品演示。

❺ I would like to express my appreciation for all your kindness during our stay in Cincinnati.

为您对我们在辛辛那提时的友好款待表示感谢。

❻ I appreciate all the time you spent showing me around your office and factory.

非常感谢您抽出时间来带领我们参观您的办公环境和厂房。

❼ I appreciate you introducing us to so many places of interest in Yantai.

感谢您向我们介绍了众多的烟台名胜。

❽ I hope that you will have a chance to visit us in Hamburg sometime soon.

希望您在不远的将来有机会来汉堡找我们。

❾ If both of our schedules permit, I would like to visit you again this summer.

如果我们双方的时间都允许的话，我想今年夏天再去拜访您。

❿ Thank you for all your kindness and support during my trip.

感谢您在我旅行期间对我的照顾和帮助。

⓫ Thank you again for your wonderful hospitality.

再次感谢您的热情款待。

信例 1

Dear Mr. Tang,
Thank you very much for your wonderful hospitality during our stay in Sichuan. We sincerely appreciate you taking time out of your busy schedule to show us around your office and factory. I hope that you will have a chance to visit us in London in the near future.
Best regards,
Jessica Hughes

非常感谢我们到四川时您对我们的热情款待。我们真心感谢您在百忙之中抽出时间带我们到您的办公室和工厂转转。我期望您能在不远的将来抽空到伦敦来找我们。

信例2

Dear Beth,

I would like to express my appreciation to you for making our trip to Boston such an enjoyable and successful one. It was a pleasure to meet with you and your colleagues, and to see your beautiful new office. The accommodations you arranged for us were excellent as well. Thank you for your warm hospitality.

Yours truly,

Veronica

您为我们安排了如此舒适顺利的波士顿之旅，对此我表示衷心的感谢。很高兴见到你和你的同事们，还参观了你漂亮的新办公室。你给我们安排的住宿也非常棒。谢谢你热情的款待。

第十四部分　组织会议
Writing about Conferences

89 邀请 Making an invitation

❶ We cordially invite you to attend the 15th Annual Conference on Applied Robotics.

我们诚挚地邀请您出席主题为机器人应用的第 15 届年会。

❷ The conference will be held on May 18 at 1:30 pm and located in Room 102 of Nicholson Hall.

本次会议将于 5 月 18 日下午 1:30 在尼科尔森大楼 102 号房间召开。

❸ Please refer to the attached brochure for a map and directions.

方位图请参见附件里的宣传册。

❹ The conference agenda is included below and can also be viewed on our website.

会议日程安排请见下文，或登陆我们的网站浏览。

❺ Professor Louis McDonald of Emerson College will be our featured guest speaker.

爱默生大学的路易斯·麦克唐纳德教授将担任我们专题的客座主讲。

❻ We would be honored if you would attend this special celebration.

如果您能出席这次特别庆典我们将感到不胜荣幸。

❼ If you would like to attend the conference, please complete the attached form and e-mail or fax it back to me by Friday, June 5.

如果您想参加此次会议，请填写附件的表格，并于 6 月 5 日（周五）之前以电子邮件或传真的形式发送给我。

❽ For further information, please refer to the attached conference agenda.

详细信息请参见附件里的大会日程。

❾ Please visit the conference website for further information.

具体信息请登陆大会网站。

❿ I hope you will be able to attend this event.

我希望你能出席这次会议。

信例1

Dear Friends,

Lion Robotics Group cordially invites you to attend the 10th Annual Symposium on Nanotechnology and Nanoscience. The symposium will be held on Monday, May 3rd at 9:00 am at the Huaxia Conference Center. Guest speakers include Dr. Min-Wei Yang of Fudan University and Professor Hiroshi Tanaka of Kyoto University. Please visit our website for further information.

Sincerely,

Yan-Jiang Hu

莱昂·罗伯蒂克斯集团诚挚地邀请您参加关于纳米科技的第十届年度研讨会。此次研讨会将于5月3日(周一)上午9:00在华夏会议中心举行。客座主讲人是复旦大学的杨民伟博士和京都大学的田中博史教授。详细情况请登陆我们的网站查询。

信例2

Dear Friends and Colleagues,

You are cordially invited to attend a special presentation to unveil Shenghua Corporation's new line of GPS watches. The presentation will be held on Wednesday, May 17 at 2:30 pm at our corporate headquarters: 10A Jianguo Road, Chaoyang District, Beijing, 100025. I look forward to seeing you all there.

Sincerely,

Ming-Jing Sun, Executive Vice President

我们诚挚地邀请您参加盛华公司关于新系列卫星定位手表的专品展示会。此次展示会将于5月17日(周三)下午2:30在公司总部举办,总部地址为:北京市朝阳区建国路10A。邮编:100025。届时期待您的光临。

90 回复邀请 Replying to an invitation

① Thank you for the invitation to attend your upcoming conference.

谢谢您邀请我参加即将召开的会议。

② I am honored to accept your invitation to attend your company's 25th anniversary event.

我很荣幸地接受您的邀请参加贵公司的25周年庆典。

❸ I would like to confirm my registration for the Automobile Designers' Conference.

我想确认我是否已经登记参加本次汽车设计师大会。

❹ Unfortunately, I will be out of town that week and hence unable to attend the conference.

很不凑巧，那一周我会在外地因此不能参加那个会议了。

❺ However, I hope that I will be able to attend next year's conference.

但我希望明年的会议我能参加。

❻ Thank you again, and I look forward to seeing you there.

再次感谢，期待届时与您见面。

信例 1

Dear Mr. Young,
Thank you very much for the invitation to attend your product launch event of July 24-25. I will likely be visiting Europe for a short business trip this summer, but the dates have not yet been determined. Assuming I'm not overseas, I will be delighted and honored to attend this event.
Best regards,
Cecil Murphy

非常感谢您邀请我参加 7 月 24 日至 25 日的新产品发布会。今年夏天我可能要去欧洲做一次短途旅行，不过具体日期还没有确定。如果我没有出国，我会很荣幸地出席发布会的。

信例 2

Dear Ms. Morgan,
Thank you for inviting me to attend your company's 15th anniversary conference and dinner on June 10th. Unfortunately, as I have a prior engagement scheduled for that afternoon, I will be unable to attend the conference. However, I will be glad to attend the dinner reception. I'm looking forward to seeing you then.
Sincerely,
Tanya Henderson

感谢您邀请我参加贵公司于 6 月 10 日举办的 15 周年纪念会和晚宴。很不巧，那天下午我已经安排了其他事情，不能出席纪念会了。不过我还是很高兴能够参加晚宴。期待届时能见到您。

91 会后交流 Post-conference contact

❶ It was a pleasure to attend your product launch of July 10.

我很高兴参加了你们于 7 月 10 日举办的产品发布会。

❷ I wanted to let you know that I thoroughly enjoyed your seminar last week.

我想告诉您我非常喜欢您上周的研讨会。

❸ I look forward to attending your conference again next year.

期待来年还能参加贵方的会议。

信例 1

Dear Melanie,

I wanted to tell you that I really enjoyed attending your company's 10th anniversary conference and celebration on Friday. We have a longstanding partnership and friendship, and it was a privilege to share in celebrating Stalagmite Corporation's achievements of the past decade. I wish you and your company every success in the future.

Best regards,

Christiana

我想告诉您，周五贵公司的 10 周年纪念庆典办得真是太好了。我们两家公司建立了长期的合作和伙伴关系，在过去的十年间对石笋公司的成就有着最切身的体会。希望您和您的公司今后也一帆风顺、马到功成！

信例 2

Dear Mr. Butler,

I am writing to let you know how much I enjoyed your seminar last weekend. In addition to learning a great deal about your company and its products, I also gained a better understanding of current trends within the industry. I look forward to attending more of your seminars in the future.

Sincerely,

Carrie Richards

我写这封信是为了告诉您我有多喜欢你们上周末的专题研讨会。我不仅对您的公司和产品有了广泛的了解，还对工业的最新发展趋势有了更好的认识。希望今后能多参加你们的研讨会。

第十五部分　贸易往来
Business Correspondence

92 咨询公司信息 Asking for information about a company

❶ I would like to request a copy of your company brochure.

我想要一份贵公司的简介。

❷ I am writing to request information about your company.

我写信是想咨询贵公司的相关信息。

❸ I am very interested in learning more about your company.

我很有兴趣想更进一步地了解贵公司。

❹ Is it possible to obtain a copy of your annual report?

您可不可以给我一份贵公司的年度报告?

❺ Thank you in advance for your kind attention.

提前感谢您的关注。

❻ I look forward to hearing from you soon.

我期待尽快收到您的回复。

信例1

Dear Sir or Madam,
I would like to request information about your company to facilitate my research for a school project. The project focuses on start-up food processing companies and their impact within the industry. I would appreciate any corporate brochures or marketing materials with which you could provide me. Thank you very much for your help.
Sincerely,
Joshua Griffin

我想向贵公司咨询一些信息,以帮助我进行一个项目研究。这个项目主要是针对食品初加工的公司以及其对该行业的影响。如果您能将一些可以公布的公司业务简介或市场销售资料提供给我,将不胜感激。非常感谢您的帮助。

To Whom It May Concern,

I'm writing to request a copy of your company's annual report. As a longtime user of your products, I'm interested in purchasing shares of your company for my investment portfolio; reviewing your annual report would enable me to make an informed decision. Thank you in advance for your assistance.

Sincerely,

MarciaPeterson

我写信给您是希望您能给我一份贵公司的年度报告。作为贵公司产品的长期使用者，我对购买一些贵公司的股份做为一项投资很感兴趣；浏览一下贵公司的年度报告可以帮助我更好的做出决定。先感谢您的帮助。

93 介绍公司 Introducing a company

❶ Thank you for inquiring about our company.　感谢您对我公司的垂询。

❷ Thank you very much for your interest in our company.　非常感谢您对我公司的关注。

❸ We are one of China's largest exporters of medical devices.　我们是中国最大的医疗设备出口商之一。

❹ We specialize in automobile, home, life, and commercial insurance.　我们专门从事汽车、家庭、人寿和商业的险种。

❺ Our company has over 30 years of experience in the plastics industry.　我公司在塑料制品业拥有 30 多年的经验。

❻ We would be glad to provide you with a copy of our company brochure.　我们很愿意送给您一份公司简介。

❼ Please visit our website for further information about our company.　关于我公司的详细信息请登陆我们的网站。

❽ If you have any further questions, please feel free to contact us again.　如还有问题请随时与我们联系。

❾ Please let us know if you have any additional questions.　如果还有其他问题请与我们联系。

❿ Thank you again for your interest in our company.　再次感谢您对我公司的关注。

⓫ We look forward to serving you in the near future.　希望在不远的将来能为您服务。

⑫ We look forward to the opportunity to serve you.　我们希望有机会为您效劳。

Dear Ms. Powell,

Thank you for your interest in our company. As per your request, we are attaching an electronic version of our corporate brochure for your review. In addition, a copy of our annual report has been mailed to the address you provided. Please feel free to contact us if you have any further questions.

Sincerely,

Manny Robinson

感谢您对我们公司的关注。根据你提出的要求，我们将公司简介的电子版文件放在附件里请您阅览。此外还有一份公司年报的副本也已寄到您所提供的地址去了。如果您还有任何问题，欢迎随时咨询我们。

Dear Mr. Fisher,

We write to introduce ourselves as a leading translation company, based in Beijing, China. Our company specializes in Asian language services, including translation between English and Chinese, Japanese, Korean, Indonesian, Vietnamese, and Thai. Please see our attached brochure for an overview of our company and a list of our rates.

Sincerely,

Hai-Dong Chen

我们写这封信是想向您毛遂自荐。我公司是一家知名的翻译公司，位于中国北京。我们主要提供亚洲区语言服务，包括英语和中文、日语、韩语、印尼语、越南语以及泰语之间的互译。公司简介和价目表请参见附件。

---

94 询问产品信息 Asking for product information

❶ I would like to request a copy of your product catalog.　我想要一份贵方产品目录。

❷ I am writing to request information about your latest products.　我想咨询一些有关贵公司新产品的信息。

❸ I am very interested in learning more about your products/services.

我很想进一步了解您的产品/服务。

❹ We are very interested in your new children's clothing line.

我们对贵公司最新的儿童服装系列非常感兴趣。

❺ Could you tell me the average battery life of your X625 laptops?

您可不可以告诉我贵公司 X625 型笔记本电脑的电池平均寿命是多长时间?

❻ Could you provide me with information on your T1000-series products?

您是否能提供贵公司生产的 T1000 系列产品的信息?

❼ What are the differences between the L100 and L125 headphones?

L100 和 L125 型头戴式耳机有哪些区别?

❽ I was wondering whether you offer free product samples.

您是否能提供一些免费的产品样品。

❾ Could you please send me some product samples?

您是否能寄给我一些产品小样?

❿ I would like to know whether discounts are available on bulk orders.

我想知道如果批量购买的话是否能有折扣。

⓫ Do you accept orders from outside of the United States?

贵公司是否接受美国以外的海外订单?

⓬ Thank you in advance for your assistance.

提前感谢您的协作。

⓭ I look forward to hearing from you soon.

期待尽快收到您的回复。

信例1

Dear Sir or Madam,
I am interested in purchasing several of your company's tea sets for my store. Could you provide me with detailed information on prices, delivery costs, and payment terms? Are discounts available for bulk orders? In addition, I would like to receive a copy of your product catalogue if possible. Thank you in advance.
Sincerely,
Ken Simmons

我想为自己的店铺购进几套贵公司的茶具。贵方可不可以提供给我一些详细信息(包括：产品价格、运送价格和支付条款)? 如果批量购买的话是否有折扣? 另外，如果可以的话，我还想要一份贵公司的产品目录。提前致以感谢。

To Whom It May Concern,
I would like to ask a couple of questions about your French language-learning software. First, what are the minimum requirements for my computer to run the software? Second, would this software be suitable for beginner-level students of French? Thank you for your time and attention. I look forward to your reply.
Sincerely,
Pamela Edwards

关于贵公司的法语学习软件我有两个问题想向您咨询。第一，要运行这套软件对电脑的最低要求是什么？第二，这套软件适合法语的初学者使用吗？感谢您关注并抽出时间看我的邮件。期待您的回复。

95 介绍产品及报价

Introducing products and quoting prices

❶ Thank you for inquiring about our products/services.

感谢您垂询我公司的产品/服务。

❷ Thank you for your interest in our products/services.

感谢您对我公司产品/服务的关注。

❸ Thank you for your interest in our food processing machines.

感谢您关注我公司的食品加工机。

❹ We would be glad to provide you with a copy of our latest product catalog.

我们很乐意向您提供一份近期的产品目录。

❺ Please visit our website for further information about our products and services.

关于我公司产品及服务项目的详细信息请登陆我们的网站。

❻ Please let us know if you would like to receive free samples of our products.

如果您想要一些我公司产品的免费小样请与我们联系。

❼ Please find attached a copy of our company brochure for your perusal.

我公司的业务介绍请参见附件。

❽ You may place your order by telephone, fax, e-mail, or regular mail.

您可以采用电话、传真、电子邮件或来函订购。

❾ As per your request, we have sent you a copy of our product brochure.

我们已按照您的要求将产品介绍手册寄出。

❿ Our halogen desk lamps are available in red, green, and blue colors.

我们的卤素台灯有红色、绿色和蓝色的。

⑪ The product you inquired about is currently on sale for 300 RMB.

您所咨询的产品目前售价为 300 元人民币。

⑫ We offer a 100% satisfaction guarantee on all of our merchandise.

我们保证我们的所有商品都能让您百分之百满意。

⑬ We offer free shipping on all orders of 200 euro or more.

所有 200 欧元以上（含 200 欧元）的订单我们都将免费寄送。

⑭ Please let us know if you have any further questions.

如有其他问题请与我们联系。

⑮ We look forward to hearing from you again soon.

我们希望能再次为您服务。

信例1

Dear Ms. Burns,

Thank you for your e-mail and your interest in our products. Our electronic dictionaries range in price from $125 to $300, with varying physical dimensions, lexicon size, and auxiliary functions. I've attached a copy of our latest product catalog for your review. If you have any further questions, please feel free to contact us.

Sincerely,

Albert Simpson

感谢您的来信以及对我们产品的关注。我们的电子辞典按照成品尺寸、词汇量和功能的不同而分为多个型号，价格区间为 125 美元至 300 美元。我把最新的产品目录单放在附件里请您阅览。如还有任何问题请随时与我们联系。

信例2

Dear Mr. Garrett,

Thank you for your inquiry regarding our new line of canned energy drinks. As you requested, I have attached our product brochure and price list for your review. Please let me know if you would like to receive complimentary samples of any of our products. I look forward to hearing from you again soon.

Sincerely,

Lorena Reynolds

感谢您对我们新推出的罐装系列能量饮品的咨询。我已经按照您的要求把产品简介和价目表放在附件里了，请您阅览。如果您想要我公司产品的赠送样品，请与我联系。期待尽快收到您的回复。

96 讨价还价 Negotiating prices

讨价 *Making an offer*

❶ Would you consider reducing the unit price from 750 RMB to 700 RMB?

可不可以把单价由 750 元降到 700 元人民币？

❷ If you are willing to offer us a 5% discount, we would be happy to place an order immediately.

如果您能给我们打个九五折，我们会很高兴地立刻下订单。

❸ Considering the large order size, I believe that a discounted price is justified.

由于我们购买的数量较多，所以我认为适当的优惠是合理的。

❹ We are very interested in establishing a long-term relationship with your company.

我们很愿意跟贵公司建立长期的合作关系。

❺ If you can lower the unit price by USD 2.00, we will increase our purchase volume to 500 units.

如果您能把单价降低两美元，我们就会把订购数量增加到 500 个。

❻ We hope that you can make a price concession on your V300 water filters.

我们希望贵公司的 V300 滤水器的价格能再优惠一些。

❼ We look forward to your positive response.

希望收到您肯定的答复。

还价 *Making a counter-offer*

❶ Based on your purchase volume, we are prepared to offer you a 2% discount.

根据您购买的数量，我们打算给您 2% 的优惠。

❷ We are pleased to offer you a unit price of CAD 125.00 on our Y365 laser circuits.

我们愿意把 Y365 激光电路的单价降到 125 加元。

❸ Given the high quality of our merchandise, we believe that this is a reasonable price.

鉴于我们的商品品质优秀，我们认为目前的价格是合理的。

❹ Unfortunately, USD 75.00 is the lowest price we can offer on this product.

不好意思，75 美元是我们所能承受的这个产品的最低价格。

❺ Please keep in mind that this price is inclusive of taxes and shipping.

请注意这个价格是包含税金和运费的。

❻ I'm afraid that we will be unable to lower our price any further.

恐怕这个价格已经不能再低了。

❼ We are confident that you will find this price reasonable.

我们相信您会发现这个价格是公道的。

信例1

Dear Mr. Nichols,

Thank you for your prompt reply. I trust that your company's editing service is of top quality. Given the large volume of text to be edited, however, I believe that a discounted price is justified. Would you consider reducing the per-word rate from $0.10 to $0.08? I look forward to your positive response.

Yours sincerely,

Roy Montgomery

感谢您迅速的回复。我坚信贵公司的编辑服务是顶尖水平。尽管贵公司编辑过大量的文本，但是我认为在价格上应该还有优惠的余地。把每个字0.1美元降到0.08美元你觉得如何？期待您能同意。

信例2

Dear Ms. Ellis,

Thank you very much for your letter. Based on your anticipated purchase volume, we are glad to offer you a 5% discount before shipping charges. Please find attached an order form, which can be either e-mailed or faxed back to us at your convenience. We look forward to the opportunity to serve you.

Best regards,

Ingrid Fletcher

非常感谢您的来信。根据您预期购买的数量，我们可以在计算运输费用之前给您打一个九五折。附件里有一个订单表，您可以用电邮回复也可以传真给我们，看您怎么方便。我们期待有机会为您服务。

97 下订单 Placing an order

❶ We are pleased to place an order with you for 1,000 cases of canned peaches.

我们想订购1000箱贵公司的蜜桃罐头。

❷ I would like to place an order for 25 of your M100 wireless microphones.

我想在贵公司订购25个M100型无线麦克风。

❸ We would appreciate it if you could ship these products to us as soon as possible.

如果您能将我们所订产品尽快送到我们将不胜感激。

❹ We hope to receive this order by the end of the month, if possible.

如果可以的话，我们希望能在月底之前收到这批货。

❺ I have attached a completed order form for this product, as requested.

我已经按照要求将填好的订单放在附件里。

❻ Please bill me using the credit card information on file from my last order.

请按照我最后一次订单上填写的信用卡信息划取货款。

❼ I will send a certified check for USD 1,025.50 by express mail this afternoon.

今天下午我会把一张 1025.50 美元的有效支票快递给你。

信例 1

Dear Mr. Meyer,

I would like to place an order to purchase 300 of your T500XL 1.5-liter cordless kettles (150 kettles in metallic black, 75 in charcoal gray, and 75 in pearl white). The completed order form is attached. Please use the credit card number and expiration date on file from my last order.

Sincerely,

Rudy Armstrong

我想下一份订单购买 300 台贵公司的 T500XL 型 1.5 升电热水壶（其中金属黑 150 个，炭灰色 75 个，珍珠白 75 个）。填好的订单请见附件。我的信用卡号和有效日期请以我最新提交的订单上提供的信息为准。

信例 2

Dear Ms. Harper,

Thank you for your reply. I appreciate the discount you have offered and would like you to go ahead with proofreading of the attached manuscript. I will remit the $50 deposit to your bank account by tomorrow morning. Do you think it will be possible to finish this job by next Friday?

Best regards,

Lance Sullivan

感谢您的回复。我对您给我的优惠很满意，同时希望您能再帮我把附件里的稿件校对一遍。明天上午我会汇 50 美元到您的账户里当作订金。下周五之前您可以完成这项工作吗？

98 确认订单 Confirming an order

① Thank you for placing an order for our dark chocolate.

感谢您订购我们的黑巧克力。

② We are writing to confirm your order for 100 feather pillows.

我们写信是想确认您关于100个羽绒枕头的订单。

③ This e-mail is to confirm your order for 2,000 pounds of California pistachios.

本信意在确认您订购的2000磅加州开心果。

④ You should receive your order within one to two weeks.

您将在一到两周内收到您订的货。

⑤ Please allow up to 10 business days for delivery.

寄送时间约为10个工作日。

⑥ We hope that you will be completely satisfied with your purchase.

希望我们的产品能让您称心如意。

⑦ We are confident that you will be satisfied with our products.

我们相信您会对我们的产品感到满意。

⑧ We appreciate your business and look forward to serving you again soon.

我们感谢您的订购，并期待不久能继续为您服务。

⑨ We hope that you will enjoy our products.

希望您喜欢我们的产品。

⑩ Thank you again for your business.

再次感谢您的购买。

信例1

Dear Ms. Walsh,

Thank you for placing an order for our handmade jewelry. Your transaction has been completed and a receipt for your purchase has been e-mailed to you. You should receive your shipment in three to four business days. We appreciate your business and hope that you will enjoy our products.

Sincerely,

Elaine Hamilton

感谢您订购我们手工制作的首饰。您的交易已经完成，收据业已发送至您的电子邮箱里。货品将于三四个工作日内送到。感谢您购买我公司商品，希望您能满意。

信例 2

Dear Mr. Jennings,
We have received your order for 100 cuckoo clocks（model A360-1）. Please allow two to three weeks for delivery. We are confident that you will be satisfied with your purchase. However, in the event that you receive any damaged or defective items, simply return them for a full refund. Thank you for your business.
Sincerely,
Saul Goodwin

我们已经收到您的订单，您订购的商品是 100 个布谷鸟闹钟（型号 A360-1）。运送时间为两至三周。我们相信您会对我们的商品感到满意。不过，您收到的物品有任何损坏或缺陷，请退回给我们，我们将给您全额退款。感谢您的购买。

99 催货 Urging delivery

❶ I placed an order last month for 1,500 bottles of your mango juice.

我上个月就订购了 1500 瓶贵公司的芒果汁。

❷ I have not yet received the computer hardware that I ordered over six weeks ago.

我 6 周以前订购的电脑硬件至今仍未收到。

❸ In your e-mail of July 8, you assured us that we would receive the goods by July 31.

您在 7 月 8 日的邮件中向我们保证过 7 月 31 日能收到货物。

❹ It has been over five weeks since I placed my order with your company.

距离我在贵公司下订单已经有 5 周多了。

❺ We are still waiting to receive our order of 30 granite kitchen tables.

我们仍未收到预订的 30 块花岗岩厨房案桌。

❻ I would appreciate it if you could expedite delivery of this shipment.

如果您能加快货物的装运我将不胜感激。

❼ Please let me know the reason for this extensive delay.

请告知延误原因。

❽ I'm afraid that we cannot afford to wait any longer for this shipment.

我恐怕不能再继续等待这批货物的装运了。

❾ Please understand that late deliveries adversely affect our sales.

请理解这次交货延误给我们的销售带来了不利影响。

❿ Please look into this matter and ship our order as soon as possible.

请调查该情况，尽快装运我们所订货物。

⓫ Thank you in advance for looking into this matter.

提前对您调查此事表示感谢。

⓬ Thank you for your attention to this matter.

感谢您对这一问题予以关注。

信例 1

Dear Ms. Vaughn,
It has been almost two months since we placed an order for 50 of your company's J-1024 scientific calculators. Several of our customers have been waiting for this product, and we are likely to lose business if we remain out-of-stock for too long. I hope that you will expedite shipment of our order.
Sincerely,
Brianna Dawson

从我们下订单当天算起现在已经将近两个月了。我们订购的是 50 部贵公司生产的 J-1024 型科学计算器。许多客户都很期待这件商品，我们不想因为商品断货太长时间而坐失商机。希望您能督促尽快发货。

信例 2

Dear Sir or Madam，
I am still waiting to receive the book "English Grammar: Past, Present and Future", which I ordered over six weeks ago. At the time of ordering, I was told that it would be shipped within two weeks, and I cannot wait indefinitely. Please ensure that this item is sent out without further delay.
Sincerely,
Anthony Baldwin

我 6 个星期以前就订购了贵公司的《英语语法：过去时、现在时和将来时》一书，至今仍未收到。订单完成时，贵处告诉我将在两周之内送货，我不能无限期的等待。请核实该书是否发出，不要再拖延了。

100 为交货延迟而道歉 Apologizing for delayed delivery

❶ We apologize for the delay in shipping your order.

我们对交货延误深感抱歉。

❷ I would like to apologize for the lengthy delay in shipping your order.

我要为交货延迟这么长时间而向您道歉。

❸ We are doing everything we can to ensure that your order is shipped without further delay.

我们已经尽了最大努力保证您所订货物的装运不会再有任何延误。

❹ We will ensure that you receive your shipment by next Monday at the latest.

我们保证最迟下周一，您将会收到所订货物。

❺ Please accept our apologies for the inconvenience we have caused you.

我们为给您造成的不便而深感抱歉，请接受我们的歉意。

❻ We are very sorry for any inconvenience this may have caused.

对给您造成的任何不便我们深感抱歉。

❼ Thank you for your understanding.

感谢您的理解。

信例 1

Dear Ms. Norris,

We are very sorry for the delay in shipping your order. The delay resulted from a glitch in our inventory system, which we have since addressed and resolved. Your shipment was sent out earlier today and you should receive it by tomorrow. Please accept our sincere apologies for any inconvenience we have caused you.

Sincerely,

Gavin Sweeney

非常抱歉我们耽误了您所订货物的运送。这次延误是因为我们的存货系统出现故障，现在问题已经解决了。今天上午我们已将您订的货物装运，预计明天能够送到。给您造成诸多不便，非常抱歉。请接受我们诚挚的歉意。

信例2

Dear Mr. Thornton,

We apologize for the extended delay in your shipment. Unfortunately, due to excessive demand last month, we were unable to fill all orders on time. We will ensure that your order is shipped immediately, and will credit your account for the full cost to compensate for your inconvenience. Thank you for your understanding.

Sincerely,

Ruth Atkins

很抱歉我们交货延迟了。不幸的是，由于上个月订单过多，我们未能按时交付所有的订单。我们保证您订的货会马上装运，给您带来的任何经济损失我们都会全额赔偿。感谢您的谅解。

101 催货款 Urging payment

❶ This is a reminder that payment for your last order has not yet been received.

提醒您尚未支付上次订单的货款。

❷ Unfortunately, we have not yet received payment for your order of August 10th.

遗憾的是，我们至今仍未收到您 8 月 10 日所下订单的货款。

❸ Please pay the outstanding balance of USD 325. 75 as soon as possible.

请尽快支付 325.75 美元的未付货款。

❹ We would appreciate prompt payment of the outstanding balance.

如能尽快付清未付账款我们将深表感谢。

❺ We look forward to receiving your favorable reply/response.

期待收到您肯定的回复。

❻ Your cooperation in this matter will be appreciated.

如能配合我们的工作，我们将不胜感激。

❼ Thank you in advance for your cooperation.

提前感谢您的合作。

Dear Mr. Freeman,

This is to remind you that payment for last month's order (Order No. 1281024) has not yet been received. As it has been over 45 days since the purchase date, we would like to ask you to pay the outstanding balance of $275.24 as soon as possible. Thank you for your cooperation.

Sincerely,

Dora Cunningham

提醒您上个月的货款还没有收到（订单号为 1281024）。自购买之日算起至今已超过 45 天，我们想请您尽快支付未付账款 275.24 美元。谢谢您的合作。

Dear Ms. Owens,

In your last e-mail, you indicated that you would be sending a check to pay your overdue account balance. Unfortunately, we have not yet received this payment. If it would be more convenient for you, secure credit card payments can also be made through our website. We appreciate your attention to this matter.

Sincerely,

Louise Perkins

您的上一封邮件中提到您已经寄出一张支票用来支付过期的账款。不幸的是，我们至今仍未收到。如果方便的话，您可以通过我们的网站用信用卡安全支付。感谢您对此事的关注。

102 请求延期付款 Requesting deferred payment

❶ I understand that payment for our last order is due next Monday.

我知道我们上次订单的账款应于下周一支付。

❷ Would it be possible to extend the payment deadline until the end of the month?

可不可以将支付期限延长到月底？

❸ We would greatly appreciate it if you could grant us a 10-day payment extension.

如果您能将付款期限推迟 10 天我们将不胜感激。

❹ I would like to apologize for the overdue balance on our account.

逾期未能付清货款我为此向您道歉。

❺ Would it be acceptable to remit payment by September 5th?

能否将支付期限延至 9 月 5 日？

❻ Thank you for your understanding.

感谢您的谅解。

信例 1

Dear Ms. Palmer,

I am terribly sorry for the overdue balance on our account. It turns out that the last invoice we received from you was somehow misplaced. Would it be possible to grant us a 10-day payment extension? I can ensure that you will receive the outstanding balance by next Friday. Thank you for your understanding.

Sincerely,

Steve Carlson

非常抱歉我们逾期未能付清账款。原来是上次您的发货单送来之后不知怎么找不到了。可不可以延长 10 天支付期限？我保证下周五之前您可以收到未付账款。感谢您的谅解。

信例 2

Dear Mr. Snyder,

We are thrilled with the recent software localization that you completed for us. I understand that payment is due within 14 days, but I was wondering whether it might be possible to extend this period by one week. Please let me know if that would be acceptable. Thank you again for your exceptional service.

Sincerely,

Hannah Tucker

您帮助我们安装调试的软件本地化工作非常成功。我知道应该在 14 天内支付您的报酬，可是您看能不能推迟一周付款？如果您同意的话请告诉我。再次感谢您优质的服务。

第十六部分　申请信函
Application Letters

103 申请职位/求职 Applying for a job

❶ I am writing to apply for the position of financial analyst at your firm.

我想申请贵公司的金融分析师一职。

❷ I would like to apply for the position of assistant engineer with your company.

我想申请贵公司的助理工程师一职。

❸ I received my B. Sc. in Biochemistry from the University of Edinburgh last year.

我去年拿到了爱丁堡大学生化系的理学士学位。

❹ I will receive a Ph. D. in Astrophysics from Stanford University this May.

我将于今年5月获得斯坦福大学的天体物理学博士学位。

❺ I possess strong leadership, communication and analytical skills.

我有较强的领导能力、沟通能力和分析能力。

❻ I possess over five years of experience in the telecommunications industry.

我有超过5年的通讯业工作经验。

❼ I believe that my portfolio of skills makes me an excellent candidate for this position.

我相信自己的相关技能使我能成为这个职位的最佳人选。

❽ In addition to my extensive accounting experience, I possess strong communication, leadership, and interpersonal skills.

我不仅拥有丰富的会计经验，还具有较强的沟通能力、领导能力和人际交往能力。

❾ Please refer to my attached résumé for a summary of my skills and experience.

关于我的专业技能和相关经验请见附件里的个人简历。

❿ Please find attached a copy of my résumé for your review.

我的简历请见附件。

⓫ I will call you in the next two weeks to arrange a time for us to meet.

我会在两周之内打电话给你商定见面的时间。

⓬ I look forward to discussing my qualifications with you in greater detail.

期待能跟您进一步详细叙述我的工作能力。

⓭ I look forward to hearing from you soon.

期待尽快收到您的回复。

⑭ Thank you very much for your time and consideration.　　　谢谢您抽出时间来对我的问题予以考虑。

⑮ Thank you for your consideration.　　　谢谢您的关注。

信例 1

Dear Mr. Spencer,

I am writing to apply for the position of junior accountant at your company.

During the past two summers, I interned at Mason & Hunt LLP in Ottawa, where I assisted in bookkeeping, auditing and corporate tax preparation. I will be receiving my BBA this May from York University, with a major in financial accounting. In addition to my work experience and solid academic background, I possess strong leadership, communication and computer skills. A copy of my résumé is attached for your review.

I would greatly appreciate the opportunity to meet with you to discuss this position in further detail. I will call you by the end of the month to arrange a time to meet. In the meantime, please let me know if you require any additional materials from me, such as transcripts or reference letters. Thank you for your time and consideration.

Sincerely,

Vanessa Wagner

我想申请贵公司的初级会计师一职。

我连续两个夏季都在位于渥太华的 Mason & Hunt LLP 公司实习，主要协助记账、查账以及纳税申报等相关工作。我将于今年 5 月获得约克大学授予的工商管理学士学位，专业是金融财会。我不仅具备工作经验和深厚的专业素质，还具有较强的领导能力、沟通能力和计算机技术。附件里是我的简历，请您阅览。

如有机会能与您会面，进一步沟通我将不胜感激。这个月底我会给您打电话商定见面时间。如果您还有任何需要我提供的个人资料，如成绩单或推荐信，请随时与我联系。感谢您抽空阅读此信并予以考虑。

信例 2

Dear Ms. Myers,

I would like to apply for the position of Software Engineer with your company as posted on your website.

After receiving a Master of Science degree in Computer Science from Oxford University, I served as Systems Developer for Digital Millennium Corporation for the past two years. During my employment, I was responsible for enhancing web security and upgrading several software applications.

In addition to being proficient in several programming languages, I possess strong leadership, communication and problem-solving capabilities. I am also fluent in Japanese. Please refer to my attached résumé for a list of my qualifications.

I am eager to speak with you further about this opportunity, as I believe there is a strong fit between my background and skills and your company's needs. I will contact you within two weeks to inquire about the status of my application. Thank you for your consideration.

Sincerely,

Lucas Rhodes

我想申请贵公司网站上公布的软件工程师一职。

我毕业于牛津大学计算机系，获理学硕士学位。前两年我供职于数字千年公司任系统开发员。在职期间主要负责加强网络安全以及多款软件的升级工作。

除了掌握多种编程语言，我还具备较强的领导才能、沟通能力和处理问题的能力。我还能流利地用日语与人交流。我所获得的资格证书请见附件。

我很期待不久能与您面谈，我相信我的专业素质和技能完全符合贵公司对于这一职位的要求。两周内我会与您联系，请您届时告知我的申请进展情况。感谢您的关注。

104 推荐信 Letters of recommendation

❶ It is my pleasure to provide this letter of recommendation for Celina Murray.

我很荣幸能为瑟琳娜·穆瑞写这封推荐信。

❷ I am honored to write this letter of recommendation on behalf of Stanley Rice.

能为斯坦利·瑞斯写推荐信我感到很荣幸。

❸ I believe that Susanna's wide-ranging skills would be a valuable asset to your company.

我坚信苏珊娜广泛的专业技能会给贵公司创造出不可估量的价值。

❹ I am confident that Franklin would make a valuable addition to any organization.

我相信弗兰克林能为任何机构创造价值。

❺ Tabitha was a model employee and it was a pleasure to have her on our team.

泰贝莎是个模范员工，我们团队为有她而骄傲。

❻ I enjoyed having Marlon as my student and I know he will make an outstanding lawyer.

马伦是我很欣赏的学生，我认为他会是个出色的律师。

❼ Should you require any further information, please feel free to contact me anytime.

如果您想了解更多的情况，请随时与我联系。

❽ Please do not hesitate to contact me if you require any further information.

如想了解更多信息请尽管与我联系。

信例 1

To Whom It May Concern,

I am honored to write this letter of recommendation on behalf of Simone Gibson.

I have known Simone for the past year, during which time she served as Assistant Marketing Manager under my direct supervision. Her responsibilities in this position included conducting marketing research, formulating marketing strategies, and ensuring implementation of our marketing plan.

Simone possesses exceptional creative and analytical skills, enabling her to produce innovative and cost-effective solutions to a range of marketing problems. Her creativity was instrumental in the success of our last product launch. In addition, Simone has demonstrated excellent teamwork and communication skills; she is gifted at leading groups and delivering presentations.

I am confident that Simone would be a valuable asset to any organization, and it is my pleasure to recommend her for employment. If you require any further information, please do not hesitate to contact me.

Sincerely,

Karen Fitzgerald

很荣幸，西蒙妮·吉布森请我来为她写推荐信。

我是去年认识西蒙妮的，那时她担任市场经理助理一职，接受我的直接领导。她主要负责进行市场调查、制定市场销售策略，以及确保营销方案的实施。

西蒙妮具有卓越的创造力和分析能力，因此在面对一系列的营销问题时，她总能想出有独创性和高成效的解决办法。我们上一次的新产品发布会得以成功，她的创造力起到了很大作用。除此以外，西蒙妮还富有团队合作精神和优秀的沟通技能；在领导团队并将自己的想法予以传达和实施方面非常有天分。

我相信西蒙妮在任何一个公司都是非常能干的人才，我很高兴能为她写这份求职推荐信。如果您有任何问题需要进一步了解，请尽管与我联系。

Dear Sir or Madam,

It is my pleasure to provide this letter of recommendation for Jeremy Schmidt as part of his application to your company.

I have known Jeremy for the past four years in my capacity as professor and academic advisor at Harvard University, where Jeremy recently completed his Ph. D. in Computational Neuroscience under my supervision. He has also served as my research assistant for the past two years.

I have been consistently impressed by Jeremy's strong academic performance, creative problem solving, and demonstrated leadership skills. In addition to receiving high praise on his dissertation, Jeremy has been the recipient of several awards, honors, and scholarships while at Harvard University.

It is my sincere belief that Jeremy's intellect, creativity and leadership ability would make him a valuable addition to your company. Should you require any further information about Jeremy, please feel free to contact me anytime.

Sincerely,

Conrad Hoffman

我很高兴能为杰里米·施密特写这封申请贵公司职位的推荐信。

我是哈佛大学的教授，过去 4 年里一直担任杰里米的导师。在我的指导下杰里米刚刚获得计算神经科学的博士学位。过去的两年间，他也一直是我的研究助理。

杰里米出色的专业素质、独具创造性的解决问题的能力，以及卓越的领导才能都给我留下了很深的印象。此外，他的毕业论文也获得了高度的好评，杰里米在哈佛大学就读期间，多次获得各种奖励、荣誉和奖学金。

我个人坚信，杰里米的聪慧、创造力和领导才能可以为贵公司创造极大的价值。关于他如果您有任何想了解的问题，请随时与我联系。

105 申请留学 Applying to study abroad

❶ I would like to apply for your two-year intensive English course.　我想申请贵校两年制的英语精讲课程。

❷ I am writing to apply for the English immersion program at the University of Birmingham.　我想申请伯明翰大学的英语研修班。

❸ I wish to apply for admission to your university as an undergraduate student next year.　我想申请明年到贵校就读大学本科的课程。

④ I am in my final year of studies at Lanzhou University, where I am pursuing a B. A. in Music.

我是一名兰州大学的大四学生，主修音乐。

⑤ I am currently in my third year of master's studies at Shanxi University.

我目前是山西大学的大三学生。

⑥ It has long been my dream to pursue English language studies at your college.

能到贵校研读英语语言学一直是我的梦想。

⑦ I am very excited about the opportunity to engage in studies at the University of Bonn.

有机会去波恩大学读书我感到非常兴奋。

⑧ As requested, I have sent two reference letters and a copy of my academic transcript by mail.

我已经遵照要求将两份推荐信和一份成绩单副本寄出。

⑨ My completed application form is attached for your review.

已填好的申请表请参见附件。

⑩ Please find attached my completed application form.

我填好的申请表请见附件。

⑪ Thank you for your consideration.

感谢您的关注。

⑫ I look forward to your reply.

期待您的回复。

信例 1

To Whom It May Concern,

I am writing to apply for the summer intensive English program at Seneca College. Currently, I am in my second year of studies at Zhejiang University, where I am pursuing a B. A. in Sociology. Having a strong interest in languages and English in particular, I participate actively in our university's linguistics club and English debate team.

I am very excited about the opportunity to study English at Seneca College. Several of my friends have attended your courses and expressed that their learning experiences were valuable and memorable. I believe that the intensive English program would enable me to enhance my English skills and, simultaneously, learn more about the culture of your country.

My completed application form is attached for your review. Please let me know if you require any additional information.

Thank you for your consideration. I look forward to your reply.

Sincerely,

Zhao-Ping Deng

我想申请塞内加学院的夏季英语精讲班。

我是浙江大学社会学系本科大学二年级的学生，出于对语言尤其是英语的浓厚兴趣，我积极参加了我们学校的语言学俱乐部和英语辩论社。

有机会到塞内加学院学习英语我感到非常激动。许多读过这个课程的朋友都告诉我，这段学习经历对他们而言非常珍贵而且难忘。我相信，这个英语精讲班能够让我的英语得到提高，同时，对贵国的文化有更深入的了解。

我填好的申请表请见附件。如果您还需要其他信息请与我联系。

感谢您的关注。期待您的回复。

信例 2

Dear Sir or Madam,

I would like to apply for admission to your university as a Master's student in Applied Economics next September.

I am currently in my fourth year of undergraduate studies at Shandong University. Upon graduating next July, I will receive a Bachelor of Arts in Economics.

It has long been my dream to pursue graduate studies at the University of Pennsylvania, an institution noted for its excellent faculty and students, and strong leadership in the field of economics. I am confident that I could contribute to and benefit from the rich academic and cultural community of your university.

As requested, I have sent two letters of recommendation, an original copy of my university transcript, and a copy of my TOEFL certificate. Please also find attached my completed application form.

Thank you very much for your consideration. I look forward to hearing from you soon.

Sincerely,

Fang-Yi Zhou

我想申请贵校明年9月开学的应用经济学硕士课程。

我现在是一名山东大学的大四学生。明年7月毕业时将会获得经济学学士学位。

能去宾夕法尼亚大学读研究生一直是我的梦想。在贵校供职的教职员工和就读的学生都相当优秀，而且贵校在经济学领域里享有盛誉。我相信我将在这富有学术和文化氛围的校园里受到熏陶，受益匪浅。

我已经按照贵校的要求，将两份推荐信、一份大学成绩单原件以及一份托福成绩单的复印件寄出。入学申请表请参见附件。

感谢您对我的申请予以考虑。期待能尽快收到您的回复。

附　录

常用连接词

比　较	正式：similarly, in comparison, equally important 非正式：again, likewise, still, in the same way, too
转　折	正式：however, nevertheless, on the contrary, in contrast, rather than, whereas 非正式：but, although, though, instead of, on the other hand, unlike
时　间	正式：eventually, formerly, subsequently 非正式：then, next, after, later, since, while
递　进	正式：furthermore, moreover, in addition, what's more 非正式：and, first, second, third, besides, also
解释说明	正式：to illustrate, in other words, in this case 非正式：for example, for instance, such as, including, like, namely, in fact
强　调	正式：in any event, to be sure, most important, above all 非正式：of course, naturally, obviously, surely, indeed, in fact, certainly
增　加	and, also, too, also, as well as, besides, moreover, furthermore, in addition, additionally, then
结　果	therefore, as a result, consequently, accordingly, so, otherwise
让　步	although, nevertheless, of course, after all, clearly, still, yet, in spite of, despite
层　次	first, in the first place, firstly, first of all; second, secondly, again, also, and, and then, equally important, further, furthermore, in addition, moreover, next, still, too; finally, last, lastly
定　义	is, refer to, mean, that is to say
观　点	from my point of view, in my opinion, although some people believe that…, I think that…, As far as I am concerned, As I see it, the way I see it
列　举	for example, such as, in particular, a case in point, for instance
总　结	in conclusion, to conclude, taking into account all the above factors, for the reasons presented above, given the factors I have just outlined, to summarize, in summary, in brief, all in all, on the whole, therefore, in my view/opinion…

商务书信常用表达法

中文	正式用法	一般用法
按照…	as per	as; according to; in accordance with
关于，至于	as to	concerning; regarding; about
附…	attached hereto	attached
一月一号的	dated January 1	of January 1
尽早	at an early date	soon; immediately; by date
尽快	at your earliest convenience	soon; by date
关于…	pertaining to/re	of; about; concerning
由于…	due to	since; because of; owing to
如上所述	as stated above	as I have said
…之前	prior to	before
请查收附上的…	please find enclosed	enclosed is/are; I am enclosing
提供（信息等）	furnish/supply（information, etc.）	give; send
不便，麻烦	inconvenience	trouble
表明	reveal	show
叙述	state	say
终止	terminate	end; stop
足够的	sufficient	enough
签名者	the undersigned	me/I

公司职位名称

Chairperson 董事长	President 总裁，总经理
Vice President 副总裁	Senior Managing Director 资深执行董事
Managing Director 执行董事，总经理	Director 董事
Senior Advisor 高级顾问	Corporate Advisor 一般顾问
Auditor 监事	General Manager 总经理
Branch Manager 部门经理	Department Manager 经理
Deputy Department Manager 副经理	Section Manager 科长
Supervisor 主任	

公司部门名称

Head Office 总公司	Branch Office 分公司、分店
Liaison Office 办事处	Office of the President 总裁室（总经理室）
Office of the Secretary（or Secretariat）秘书室	Personnel 人事部
Human Resources 人才资源部	Accounting（or Accounts）会计部
Research and Development 研究开发部	Domestic Sales 国内销售部
Overseas Sales 国外销售部	Marketing 市场部
Materials 材料部	Purchasing（or Procurement）采购部
Production Control 生产管理处	Quality Control 质量管理部
Logistics 后勤部	Maintenance 维修部
Public Relations 公关部	Documentation 文件、资料室
Legal 法律处	Export 出口部
Overseas Operations 国外业务部	Finance 财务部
General Administration（or General Affairs）总务部	

常用信尾结束语

信尾结束语实例			
私人书信	Love, With love, Fondly, Warm regards, Thank you, With appreciation, As ever,	All my love, Lots of love, Affectionately, With all my heart, Many thanks, Missing you, Best regards,	Love and kisses, Loving you, Warmly, Forever yours, Thanks again, Your friends,
商务书信	Yours truly, Sincerely, Cordially, Best regards, With anticipation, Yours faithfully,	Yours very truly, Sincerely yours, Cordially yours, Expectantly, Formerly yours,	Very truly yours, Yours sincerely, Yours cordially, Impatiently, Faithfully yours,

常用 E-mail 表情符号

:-) or :)	笑脸："I'm joking." or "Have a nice day." or "Good luck."
:-(or :(	悲伤…；失败…；遗憾…
:-o	惊讶；震惊
:-D	微笑；大笑
:-<	生气
{} or []	拥抱（亲热的表现）
{{{***}}}	拥抱和亲吻
(^-^)	微笑
(^-*)	眨眼
<(^o^)>	哇
(?-?)	咦?
(>o<)	遭了
x _ x	好痛

图书在版编目（CIP）数据

英文 E-mail 写作 100 主题／（加）杜鲁门（Trueman, M.）著. —北京：外文出版社，2008

ISBN 978 - 7 - 119 - 05331 - 8

Ⅰ. 英… Ⅱ. 杜… Ⅲ. 电子邮件-英语-写作 Ⅳ. H315

中国版本图书馆 CIP 数据核字（2008）第 045068 号

英语国际人

英文 E-mail 写作 100 主题

作　　者	Matthew Trueman	
翻　　译	葛　欣　王　欢	

策　　划	蔡　箐
责任编辑	李春英
封面设计	红十月设计室
印刷监制	冯　浩

ⓒ外文出版社

出版发行　外文出版社

地　　址　中国北京西城区百万庄大街 24 号　　邮政编码　100037

网　　址　http://www.flp.com.cn

电　　话　（010）68995964/68995883（编辑部）
　　　　　（010）68320579/68996067（总编室）
　　　　　（010）68995844/68995852（发行部/门市邮购）
　　　　　（010）68327750/68996164（版权部）

电子信箱　info@flp.com.cn/sales@flp.com.cn

印　　制　北京蓝空印刷厂

经　　销　新华书店/外文书店

开　　本	小 16 开		印　　张	11
装　　别	平		字　　数	180 千字
版　　次	2009 年第 1 版第 3 次印刷			
书　　号	ISBN 978 - 7 - 119 - 05331 - 8			
定　　价	22.00 元			